TWO BROTHERS AT WAR

Harry Ball has written an exciting and graphic account of his life during World War Two. Sergeant Ball spent the war years as an air gunner and wireless operator in Halifax bombers and then as a prisoner in German POW camps. The scope of his narrative is widened by comparison of his experiences with those of his brother who served as a Flight Lieutenant.

We relive the tension and camaraderie of a bombing crew in action as they strain every nerve to achieve the ultimate performance possible from man and machine. Then the inevitable happens; one night they don't return.

The pain and anxiety of mothers, wives and girlfriends left at home is recreated by a skilful mixture of original letters, poetry and narrative. This is counterpointed by a vivid evocation of life in German POW camps followed by the long, harrowing march home to freedom in 1945.

For the Family

TWO BROTHERS AT WAR

Harry Ball

JANUS PUBLISHING COMPANY
London, England

First published in Great Britain 1992 by
Janus Publishing Company

Requiem for a Rear Gunner

**British Library Cataloguing-in-Publication
Data.
A catalogue record for this book is available
from the British Library**

ISBN 1 85756 016 7

Cover design David Murphy

Phototypeset by Intype, London

Printed and bound in England by
Antony Rowe Ltd., Chippenham, Wiltshire

Contents

Introduction

Everyone has memories which live in their minds when others have faded or vanished. For those who lived through the Second World War, memories of that war, I suspect, would be among the last to die. This would be especially true of those on active service.

My brother and I share memories which live so strongly in our minds that they really belong on paper. In our case they are memories of life in the RAF as members of Bomber Command. What happened to us, and what I have been told by others who shared similar experiences, I will never forget. I hope, therefore, that these pages will give the reader an insight into the ups and downs of the life we led and what it was like to be *two brothers at war*. But the book is also about the same two brothers before and after that war.

In writing a book like this you are aware that you are treading ground that has been covered before. There is a subconscious urge, I suppose, to say something different or to present your story from a different angle or in a way that hasn't been done before. However, I have come to the conclusion – not least because of my many conversations with wartime comrades – that this is not really a problem because what you write is bound to be different. By this I mean that every surviving crew member seems to have a different tale to tell. Indeed, one of the joys of the various RAF and other reunion meetings which happen periodically, is that people invariably have a story to relate which will surprise you.

But there are, of course, similarities too. There was the discipline and sense of urgency which came from intensive training. And those who took part in the bombing raids will speak of the camaraderie which grew up between the members of each seven-man crew. Each crew member tended to develop a strong sense of responsibility for the other six. Each had a vital but slightly different job to do, but you knew that if you did your job well the other six would have a better chance of doing their jobs well.

For me, the war was split into three distinct phases. There was training (at times this seemed interminable); action, an intense burst of it in 1943; and, finally, imprisonment in various German POW camps.

There were so many people in these camps that it was impossible to get to know more than a small number of them. But the same spirit was there. A spirit of defiance and a determination not to make things easy for the enemy. I am privileged to be able to describe what POW life was like under the leadership of the remarkable Dixie Deans (to whose exploits I will refer on several occasions). That leadership extended to a long march through East Germany before freedom came for us in May 1945.

Brother Fred's career (Flight Lieutenant Ball, 44 (Rhodesia) Squadron, RAF Waddington and 49 Squadron, RAF Scampton and Fiskerton) was going strong well before I even started. Indeed, I was able to send him a telegram of congratulations for the award of his DFC months before my own flight in anger. But I have been able, where possible, to compare and contrast his experiences and exploits with my own.

Bomber command was an arm of the services which suffered proportionately greater losses than any other. This made things particularly hard for those left behind. The dreaded telegrams telling people that their sons and loved ones were missing, presumed dead, were the worst that could be received. But the mothers and wives and girlfriends must have died a little *every* night while they simply waited to see whether their boys would come back. I have included some letters and poems which I hope give an indication of the stress they must have been under.

Other war poems are included – some by RAF servicemen and some by army servicemen – and the reader might wish to judge whether life as a desert rat had any similarities to that of a rear gunner in a Halifax or Lancaster bomber.

1

Family

My parents lived in Harrogate, Yorkshire, in the depression years of the 1920s and 30s. My story really begins in the earliest of those years. The eldest of the family, Fred, was born in 1920, and I was born two years later. We were from a working class family, my mother was cook and dad night porter at the White Hart Hotel, Harrogate.

Harrogate was a spa town, and there was plenty of hotel work about – the wages were poor, but a lot of young girls who came from out of town managed to find husbands. During the season the town was usually full of holidaymakers taking the mineral waters.

Mum and dad married in 1919, a year after the First World War. Dad had rheumatic fever twice before the age of 14; the doctors told his mother the chances were that he wouldn't live until the age of 20, but he died at 58. We lived in a rented two-up, two-down terraced house; the toilets and water were outside. Most years during the winter the pipes froze and dad had to get his blowlamp out. Dad got ten shillings a week disability pension and although later on he worked as a painter and decorator he was ill and off work a lot, so mother went out to work. My sister Marjorie was born in 1925.

It was hard for mother bringing up three children and having to get up for work at six in the morning, scrubbing floors at one of our large grocery shops. Money was very tight for us; it seemed that there were two types of people – those with and those without.

In those days there wasn't much in the way of entertainment; we had to make our own. Mother used to teach us to knit, darn, sew, and even crochet, to keep our minds occupied. Dad used to teach us paperhanging and wood graining, repairing shoes, and making bundles of firewood in an old baking tin.

At the age of about ten I was able to adapt myself to making money; I made myself a wheelbarrow out of an old pram, and used to go around the back of shops asking for old boxes, etc. Most of the shopkeepers were glad to get rid of things. I worked up a regular round, and sold eight or nine sacks a week at a shilling a sack; even in those days I was able to look after myself; I would go to the shops and buy half a dozen eggs, and half a pound of bacon, and have a good tuck in.

My parents had to do all sorts of things to make ends meet. At the grocers we used to ask for three pennyworth of broken biscuits, or stale cakes from the day before, and three pennyworth of bits of bacon from the end of joints. My favourite food was mutton bones made into a stew, and picking the bones afterwards. Although times were hard I don't think we ever did without.

I do not feel I can tell my story fully without including this background information about my family in the early days.

Brother Fred was not quite so active as I was; he used to play chess a lot – a game I could not get into. When Monopoly first came out, Fred and his pal Cliff bought it between them; Totopoly and Bull and Bears came out later.

The only time we went to the seaside was with the Sunday School; there was a trip once a year, usually to Redcar, Bridlington, or Scarborough. Also, each year the poor children were taken to the Crown Hotel for a party. Each of us was given a pair of slippers; an apple and orange, and a bag of sweets; after the party we used to slide about on the hotel dance floor in our new slippers.

A woman welfare worker came round every two or three weeks and brought us Balm cakes. Her name was Miss Vikerman, a very nice woman.

At this stage I think it would be a good idea to say more about my mother; she was a homely sort of person who always had an open house, and would help anyone who was in trouble and wanted a shoulder to cry on. Mother was a miner's daughter from Derbyshire who came to Harrogate to find work, as most of the young girls did from places like Newcastle and Durham; of course they came to find husbands as well.

Mother's idea of a good time was a seat in the 'picture house' with a quarter-pound block of Cadbury's nut milk chocolate on her lap. Each week she used to get her reading books, the magazine 'Betty's Paper' and weekend novels. Of course, a lot of this rubbed off on me; I used to go to the pictures, eat a lot of chocolate, and even read her books.

I won second prize in a film star contest in one of her books; each week six pictures of film stars were published with only part of their faces showing, and you had to guess their names; this went on for six weeks so that 36 film stars were shown in all. First prize was £10 and second prize £5. I shared my £5 with two other second prize winners and thus received £1 13s 4d. I was nine years old and had identified 31 films stars out of 36.

Early in the 1914–18 war, mother had been courting a soldier who tragically died in the conflict; this affected her nerves seriously.

Mother and father worked together in a Birmingham hotel, where they eventually became engaged.

Dad decided to look for work in Harrogate, Yorkshire, and that is how they both came to work at the White Hart Hotel. Harrogate was a spa town with work readily available in the impoverished 1920s. Our two-up and two-down house had little comfort in comparison with today.

Dad was a lot of trouble to mother mainly because of his heart; he drank quite a lot, too, and in later years they separated a few times. Harrogate was a nice town; and where we lived in the centre you could be out in the country by travelling a mile in any direction.

In the peak period when cinema-going became very popular, Harrogate had five – the Odeon, St James', Scarla, Central and the Ritz. By 1991 there was only one – the Odeon – left. Both mum and dad never showed their feelings towards each other. That is probably why I am the same with my own family, but it did not mean the feelings were not there.

In 1933 Harrogate County Council decided to pull down the old property in which we lived, so we were given notice to move.

Apart from our street, Chapel Court, Northumberland Court, Ship Yard, Union Street, and Denmark Street were the main ones; most of the families moved into council houses, on the Oakdale Estate, Ripon Road, and Bilton.

My parents were unlucky when we were leaving our house. Two of dad's so-called friends – brothers who were self-employed decorators, asked if they could stay in the house until the builders arrived. Of course, dad, like a fool, gave them the keys when we moved; when the brothers were asked to leave they refused. In the end they were given £50 for the keys, which was a lot of money in those days; they could have given dad a few pounds – we had lived there for ten years. We managed to rent a four-bedroomed house a few hundred yards from where we had lived.

As far as I know, Woolworths bought the land, which was off the main street – Oxford Street. The house we rented was 16 Mount Parade, just behind the opera house. At one end of Oxford Street was St Peter's School, which was pulled down later and the Regal Cinema was built in its place; at the other was the opera house and bus and railway stations.

2

School Days and Early Working Days

At the age of 11 I went from the junior school to Christ Church School where I stayed until I was 14. At about this time I used to get a lot of migraine headaches at school; I would stay away one or two half days a week, but eventually I grew out of it. After a short while we moved to 18 Mount Parade; here I met a new range of friends, the best one being Leslie Kilpatrick; we were like brothers and went everywhere together. We even got the chop together the same week in the RAF – he was reported killed and I missing believed killed. He was 6ft and I 5ft 2 in – most unusual pals. Our photographs were published in the Harrogate papers together. His mother and step-father had a butcher's shop in Thirsk, 22 miles away. He spent most of his time at our house even when he was on leave from the RAF.

When my brother was 14 years old, he was top boy at the school; nobody suggested that he should go to a secondary or grammar school; it seems as if working class children never got the chances they do today.

Fred's first job was at a bakery; later he managed to get an apprenticeship as a motor mechanic.

Mother ran a boarding house at Mount Parade – bed and break-fast or full board. We were now a little better off even though mother had to do most of the work. I remember at one time we had 17 teenagers staying with us from the Empire Theatre. They were taking part in a pantomime; I don't know where mother put them – four or five in a bed, I should think. Each year, different groups came to Harrogate round about Christmas time, and as we were near the theatre we got our fair share of 'guests' – I think that is a better word than 'lodgers'. As they had very little money mother only charged them five shillings per week for their bed.

I left school when I was 14; though I had not done as well as my brother, I was close to the top of the class at woodwork, painting, and handicraft. If I remember right I was twelfth in the class. Fred had the brains. School never agreed with me; what with having headaches, and often being scared of the teachers (who used to try and humiliate you when they got the chance). The youth of today would not have put up with it.

It was inevitable that I should go into decorating with my dad. Now he was what you could call a slogger, slow but sure, and always made a good job of what he was doing. He was a bit of an odd-job man as well, repairing shoes, gardening – he could put his hand to almost anything, even making wines, etc. Me? Well I was almost the opposite in some ways. I did a reasonable job but I used to do it fast, and when I worked with dad, he kept on saying: slow down, if you do the job too quickly the customer won't pay you. In those days I was quite docile, the sort of person who didn't like crowds, and tried to avoid all trouble if I could – after all I was only about five foot tall when I was 17 and I looked about 14.

Fred joined the air force six months before the war started; he went to Cardington and started his training as U/T (under training) aircrew. I tried to join as well when I was 17 ¾ years old but they told me to come back when I had grown a bit. I was 5ft tall, and you had to be 5ft 2in and 35 inches round the chest.

The youngest in the family, Beryl, was born in 1938. My sister Marjorie left school when she was 14 years old and started work as an usherette at the Central Cinema. I had seen my first talkie film there years before – Al Jolson in 'The Jazz Singer'.

Except for hotel and shop work there was very little in the way of good jobs. Of course, later on in the war Marjorie went on war work, making metal runways for Russia, at the local steel works.

I tried again to join the air force and they told me to come back when I was 18.

Fred had a bit of bad luck at Cardington in March 1939; he was confined to sick bay with scarlet fever. There was an epidemic and many of the camp personnel caught it. When rubber tubes were put in the back of his hands and arms to get the fluid out, due to an abcess in the elbow, it damaged the muscle of his left arm and he could not straighten it properly; all the time he was worried that he would not pass his medical for aircrew. He had to stay in hospital for quite a time.

Ten billets were isolated, sick quarters were overloaded with patients, and the nearby cottage hospital took the overflow. Later he was moved to a hospital in Halton for three months' electrical and massage treatment. He was moved again in August 1939 to release beds for possible war casualties. When war broke out in September 1939 I tried to join up again. I was only 5 ft 1 in tall so I was turned down again. Fred was put on six months' light administrative duties; the medical board said he wouldn't be able to go flying, so that was it, he thought, for aircrew.

In 1940 he was posted to Yatesbury on a wireless course, and to his surprise, half way through, he passed his medical for air-crew. About a year had now passed since he first joined up. After about another six months he was posted to West Freugh in Scotland on a gunnery course.

In between trying to join up I went on to the dole for a while, and was given a most interesting job by the council, guarding an aquaduct over a river at Masham in Yorkshire. Across the bridge were several pipes which supplied most of the water to Harrogate.

By this time the town was getting very busy with the army camp for the British expeditionary force (BEF) part of the air minis-try, and the Post Office Savings Bank. A group of young lads about my own age, 18 years, some were Sea Cadets, the rest most likely waiting to be called up, were given the job of guarding the bridge, twenty-four hours a day, four hours on four hours off. We did our own cooking and lived in a small hut; every week the council workmen brought us a box of groceries.

We were given scout poles and walked up and down the bridge like tin soldiers. Later on, the council sent us, believe it or not, Winchester repeaters. The barrels had been sawn off so they would not fire; heaven alone knows where they had got them from.

As we were in an isolated place, there wasn't much in the way of entertainment – just a small radio we used to listen to at a farm nearby. The farmer lived on his own so he was glad of our company.

Once a year the farmers were allowed to kill one pig for their own use, so we were at the right place at the right time. What with rationing, etc., we had plenty of bacon and meat at the meals he gave us. If I remember correctly, we were given wages of seven shillings a week – and we were there quite a few weeks. But I still wanted to get into the RAF, so I went back home.

My pal, Leslie Kilpatrick, had a grannie who lived near us. She had a boarding house, and one of her guests died and left her the lease on the Hambleton Hotel, Sutton Bank, a few miles from Thirsk; we used to cycle from Harrogate and stay there. I understand they had a dummy Spitfire squadron there during the war – the planes were made of wood.

People like Amy Johnson used to go gliding there before the war. On our way there we passed three RAF stations – Leeming, Topcliffe, and Dishforth.

I saw my first four-engined bomber there – the Halifax – never thinking I would be flying on ops in them, but I still wasn't in the RAF; I had the feeling they did not want me. At least I was keen – three times they had failed me. Fred was soon posted to Cottesmore near Oakham, where he was doing his OTU (Operational Training Unit) on Hampden bombers.

In Harrogate we hardly knew there was a war on – only that more people were living here now. The only air raid we had was launched by a lone German plane which was probably lost, and dropped its bombs on the biggest building it could find – the Majestic Hotel. A 1000 lb bomb hit its roof but did not go off; a cottage was, however, demolished on Ripon Road, and we had four windows blow out on Mount Parade; no-one was hurt. It was rumoured at the time that a rich family was staying there. Dad was the air raid warden of the district – also staff painter and night porter at the Spa Hotel, near the Majestic. When you think of what towns like London had to put up with, it is no wonder a lot of Londoners came to Harrogate; they avoided the bombing, and many of them stayed on after the war.

My fourth try to get into the RAF (I was 5ft 1⅝in tall) was unsuccessful. Again, I wasn't regarded as tall enough. I was now getting worried that I might be conscripted into the army.

Instead of going back to decorating, I took another job. I became a time keeper's assistant for Sir Lindsey Parkinson – the contractor building the army camp at Penny Pot Lane, about two miles from Harrogate. Most of the soldiers who trained there were from the BEF. They were the first to go to France, and probably got caught up in the fighting at Dunkirk.

My job was to check the hours the men had worked by going round to all the foremen each morning – joiners, steel erectors, painters, bricklayers, etc. – also paying out their wages. This work was alright when the weather was good, but it got very muddy when it rained. My next job (doing the same type of work) was for the new Post Office Savings Bank. We called it the hutments. The bank employed a surprising number of locals. When that job was finished I was transferred to Northallerton, and carried out the same work for a war emergency hospital.

I stayed at a boarding house; this was the second time I had been away from home. By now Fred was a sergeant and was posted from OTU to 44 Squadron, Waddington, flying Hampdens. He made his first trip on 12th March, 1941. About the same time I went to Cardington for the fifth time and they accepted me into the RAF. I was just 5ft 2in tall when I passed my medical. After the doctor had looked me up and down, he said, 'boy you're certainly a bantam'. Now my most important aim was to pass for aircrew.

The interviewing officer asked me what I wanted to do in the RAF. I said I wanted to be a wireless air gunner. He then said: 'why wouldn't you like to be a pilot?' I told him I would never pass the exams and that, anyway my brother was already on Ops as a Wop/AG, and if he could do it so could I. During the medical they found that my legs were too short for me to be a pilot. Out of the blue the officer said: 'what is 'Q' in morse code?' Almost straight away I said 'dash-dash-dot-dash'. He was surprised; my brother had been teaching me when he came home on leave. After that I did not get a written exam, although I should have done.

3

RAF Basic Training

The officer passed me for aircrew in March 1941. I was given a Service No. (1435132) and an identity card, and sent home on deferred service. In the meantime, I took up decorating again with dad and a Mr Weatherhead. I was now 19 years old and still waiting to be called to the RAF. As a matter of interest, when I was at Cardington, the chap in the next bed had the same name as me, and the one on the other side had the same birthday as me, 16th February 1922.

Fred was doing well by this time; he was well into his first tour, a tour being 30 trips. As only ten men out of every 100 finished one tour, and only two of these ten managed to finish a second tour, this was a hard task. We were also told that anyone managing to do four or five trips had a good chance of finishing a tour. Fred flew Hampdens as a wireless operator and gunner. He went to most of the main targets in the Ruhr area of Germany and of course the 'Big City', Berlin. He was involved in bombing, mine-laying and even dropping leaflets.

In October 1941, the RAF sent for me, and I was given a 16 week posting to Blackpool. All the aircrew under training wore a white flash in their caps. We were boarded out at Charnley Road near Blackpool Central Station. Our basic training included foot slogging, route marches, and such things as how to use the Lee Enfield rifle. In between we went to school to learn the morse code, and the use of the wireless set. After the first week 15 out of 45 had to cease training because they failed their morse test (four words a minute). They were called temperamentally unsuitable. In the Blackpool Tower ballroom we were given our inoculations (25%) afterwards we had to do PT. Two of the lads collapsed. An officer was giving us a lecture (and we were all sat down) when the injection affected me; if I had been standing I would have fallen down. For some reason I did not get the other 75% of my inoculations. In later years, my son was to ask where we got our drive from, and whether we were scared of what we were doing. The only answer I could give him was that I was more scared to fail. We were young and green, and a lot of the statistics were kept away from us. But even if we had known once we started ops that we had only three to six weeks to live, I don't think it would have made any difference. Most of the chaps who failed their wireless course became rear- or mid-upper gunners.

A lad named Taffy Gibbs went as one such gunner. The next time I saw him, we were both in a POW camp in East Prussia. He was killed later on by our own aircraft, Typhoon fighter bombers, when we were on a forced march in Germany in 1945.

All aircraft were air tested before they went on ops; two of Fred's crew were killed during an air test when a Spitfire crashed into the back of their Hampden; the Spitfire pilot was also killed.

RAF Waddington was bombed during the summer of 1941; a shelter was hit and ten people were killed, including NAAFI girls, WAAFs, and aircrew. Fred's room mate had been standing in the entrance of the shelter but was unharmed.

One night whilst Fred was in bed enemy bombers attacked the airfield; one stick of four bombs landed in a field behind the sergeants' mess; after the first drop he went into a shelter under the mess; when it was all over he found his room had been hit by shrapnel in several places. One piece went through the wall just over his bed; if he had been sitting up in bed it would have hit him.

When Fred had finished his tour and taken some leave, he was posted to Cottesmore as a flying wireless instructor. After 30 trips he needed the rest.

Back to Blackpool. We marched all over the town in squads; when the nights got darker two men had to march in front of each squad carrying a white lantern and two at the back carrying a red one.

During the day we had to attend classes, mostly aimed at increasing our morse code speed. The exam room was over a branch of Burton, the tailors; the radiators were always on, and the heat did not help any when you were doing a morse test at 20 words a minute; maybe it was done deliberately to keep you under pressure.

We did a lot of drill in Stanley Park; just inside the entrance was our armoury and one night I was on guard duty there; at the entrance gates was a sentry box, and one of my mates was on guard there; his duty was to challenge everyone who wanted to pass through, and, at the same time, let me know so I wouldn't be taken unawares, but that night he had a girl with him in the box. When an officer arrived he managed to push the girl inside the box and he got away without her being seen. The trouble was he didn't warn me: the officer walked right through the gates and armoury without being challenged; we got a good telling off, and warned what could have happened if it had been the enemy. As a matter of interest this mate of mine failed his course.

My first pay was ten shillings a week; a further shilling a day was sent to my mother. She would never spend it, but put it in the Post Office so that it was ready for me when I came home on leave.

It was just a formality really, so that if anything happened to me she would get a pension. It was a good thing we were kept busy all the time. Ten shillings a week would not have gone very far in Blackpool.

We used to play cards a lot in the billet, but I was lucky; I would never go broke because I always kept sixpence in my pocket, and nothing would tempt me to spend it.

It was two shillings to get into the Tower, or Winter Gardens, for servicemen and women who wanted to dance.

I'm afraid dancing was one of my weaknesses; the WAAFs used to try and drag me on to the dance floor, but it was no use; I just could not take to it. As we were there during the winter months we couldn't go swimming or sunbathing, although we did PT on the sands, and went to the Darby Baths. I was very nervous when we went in for morse tests and exams, but I had a guardian angel, and always managed to scrape through.

After leave I was posted to wireless school in Yatesbury, Wiltshire. This is where the hard work started, and we got our first chance to fly. It was now 1942; the RAF had started the 1000 bomber raids and brother Fred was right in the middle of it. He was posted to 49 Squadron, Scampton, on Lancaster bombers. Fred was still going out with that girl from Lincoln, Edna; he eventually married her. Also, his motorbike was still going strong – a new 150 cc Imperial. I mention this because it comes into the story later on.

Back to Yatesbury. When we first arrived everyone was talking about Flight Sergeant Hannah; he had just got the VC for saving his crew and plane over Germany by putting out a fire on the plane. He was one of our wireless instructors.

Once we started work, we had a busy schedule; it was like going to school all over again; we had examinations in wireless, practical and theory, on ground and air transmitters and receivers and also on morse code where we had to pass tests at 14/16/18 words a minute.

We had lectures on small arms: 303 rifle, sten guns, Mills bombs, and the Browning machine gun which was used in the aircraft. Also the practical side of it: firing on the range.

We had our share of route marches, cross country runs, and of course PT. And just to finish us off we had unarmed combat.

This sort of activity didn't bother me much; it was the theory side of wireless that I had a bit of trouble with. I could use my hands better than my brains, but I always managed to scrape through, despite having only had an elementary school education.

I remember that once we had a ten minute break between lessons which usually took place in the huts; when the bell rang all the classes came out together and made one mad rush for the NAAFI to get our tea and a wod (a cake, bun or doughnut); almost every squad I was in I was sure to be the smallest. This particular time I managed to get in front but fell near the entrance; everybody scrambled over me. I got hold of a drainpipe and pulled myself up – 'missed me that time'.

On the odd occasions, when we got weekend passes, a group of us used to go to Bath, a spa town very similar to Harrogate – nice scenery but not a lot to do.

I had no difficulty in passing my morse tests; we had to get up to 20 words a minute, I got 'A's most of the time, except once

when I was on 24 hour guard duty guarding the Proctor aircraft
we were flying in. The planes were tied down on the runway, but
we had been getting some strong winds. I had gone partly deaf
through a bad head cold. The next day I had a morse test and got
a 'C' – not fair really. As a reward I got a week of morse at night
class. The instructor said it wouldn't do me any harm.

Great excitement. We were told we were going flying for the
first time, on 'Proctors', single-engine aircraft. Everyone was nervous at first, but it is surprising how soon you get used to it,
looking down below you, all the fields and towns. It was like
being in a new world. Having said that, I *was* sick, but I managed
to get some work done on my 'Marconi Set'.

Our job was to get in touch with base, and ground wireless
stations all over the country, using our morse key. We had to
make out a log which was inspected after every trip; later we flew
in Dominie dragonflies, byplanes with spats on the wheels; of
course, I was sick again; I was getting a bit worried. But after
those two occasions I was never sick again while flying.

After about three months I had passed all my exams, and was
ready for posting. I went on leave to Harrogate; the town was
pretty much the same except that there were a lot more service
people about.

My pal Leslie who was 2½ years younger than me was still
waiting to get into the airforce. We did a lot of pub crawling; that
was the usual thing to do in those days.

We cycled to Sutton Bank and saw his parents who were staying
there; just for something to do we sold tea and cakes at a small
hut which was on the top of the hill; before the war it was used
for motor bike racing; the bank was very steep. During the war
they had a dummy fighter station there, with planes made out of
wood.

My next posting was a surprise – an operational squadron,
flying Wellington bombers, at Feltwell, near Mildenhall, in
Suffolk.

I wasn't going on ops; as part of my training, I had to work
with the ground wireless mechanics doing daily inspections on
Wellingtons – getting them ready for ops.

One night when a raid was on we were watching the planes
take off, when a fully-loaded Wellington ploughed into the ground
and exploded in a ball of fire.

A few days later I had to go from Feltwell to the funeral at Mildenhall, about two miles away; I had never been to a funeral like this before, doing a slow march with a squad of men and keeping in step; it was very emotional. Two of the chaps collapsed; at the time it never entered my head that I might end up the same way as this crew.

Most of our time was spent in the wireless section repairing the sets. It was a god job. I was only a few weeks at Feltwell; it was getting hard to take – seeing the aircrew taking off, and wondering how long it was going to be before I was going to fly with them. I was lucky really I had no general duties to do. At this particular time with the conversion from two-engine to four-engine bombers, and as there were loads of aircrew coming from Canada and America, our training was a bit longer than usual.

The powers that be had decided to produce a grade 1 wireless operator for two-engine bombers, although normally only four-engine bombers had a grade 1 wireless operator.

We had to leave Feltwell in a hurry as the Americans were taking over with their Bostons and Venturas; after leave, I was posted to Cranwell near Lincoln on a wireless maintenance course, and a part navigational course. It sounded good – 'Officers' Training College' – but I was only attached to it, at No. 1 Wireless School.

We had all sorts to learn: aircraft to ship semaphore with flags, as well as how to employ the Aldis Lamp, which was used all the time; air and ground wireless transmitters and receivers (British and American), Marconi and Bendix.

We were in barracks; the bedrooms were large with polished floors, about 20 men to each room. We had to take off our shoes before we entered, step on to small felt mats, and slide across the floor to our beds; the word 'Bull' meant a lot in this place.

We did the usual cross-country runs, and marching in squads on the parade ground. The warrant officer in charge always carried a baton with him; when he was mad he waved it about in the air. He used to shout out four or five orders at once like the Americans do; every so often he would call out one of the chaps to take over the squad and give orders. I was lucky; being small and in the middle of the squad, I was never called. Mind you, I was shaking in my boots all the time: at 5ft 2 in, I was hardly the sergeant-major type.

While I was at Cranwell I went over to Ruskin Avenue, Lincoln, where I was introduced to Edna and her parents; by this time she and Fred were engaged. Fred was still at Scampton, flying Lancasters. Some of the trips were long and dangerous such as the ones across the alps to Italy, which usually took nine to ten hours. The main targets were Milan, Turin and Genoa; his luck was holding out.

Back to Cranwell where we started our maintenance course. Part of our test was to make a wireless set, and get in touch with the BBC. This was a lot easier than it sounds; on the wall of the classroom was a complete diagram of the set, showing all the parts. All we had to do was put all the valves and resistors together.

On a Wellington bomber the wireless aerial was a stainless steel wire which was lowered down below the aircraft. Lead weights or balls were at the end of the wire to hold it down. One of our tests involved repairing and splicing the wire. No matter what the job, the instructor would say: 'as soon as you have finished bring it out to me to examine'. This sort of thing was a piece of cake to me; I was nearly always the first one out. It was the theory side I had trouble with. I think if my exams had been based on theory alone, I would have failed my course. I always made it up on the practical side – and that was, after all, what really counted when you were on ops.

On the 24th October 1942 Fred went on a daylight raid on Milan, flying at 300 ft to avoid radar pick up. Over the Bay of Biscay the aeroplane developed engine trouble and dived towards the sea. Because of this emergency they had to return to base.

Fred's crew were leading six Lancasters in formation from 49 Squadron, followed by another six from 97 Squadron. Years later Fred met a squadron leader who said he saw his plane go down, and thought his crew had got the chop.

After I passed out at Cranwell, it was leave again and back to Harrogate. I don't know what people must have thought with me still with a white flash in my cap. Fred's training had been about six months, then he'd gone on ops. I had been in the RAF a year already and still had a long way to go to finish my training.

4

Still Training

Marston Moor Conversion Unit – from Wellingtons to Halifaxes

After leave I was posted back to Yatesbury on a refresher course. This time we had a lot more things to do, including getting our morse speed up to 22 words a minute, and the same routine all over again. Parachute training was on the agenda – mainly how to fall when you hit the ground. You just doubled up and fell over – it was like jumping off a 15 ft wall. We were even shown how to put a chute together after it had opened. Little did I know at the time, I would have to bale out twice – once over our station at Lissett and once over Berlin. It was so easy to break your ankle or legs.

I was lucky the first time – it was a soft ploughed field; and over Berlin a dyke. During our training, the instructors gave us an idea of what it was like in a 'gas attack'. Gas pellets were placed in a cannister inside the hut and each group entered the hut with their gas masks on. Then the gas was released after we had taken our masks off. We did not stay there very long. It is funny really; Fred didn't have to do either of these things. Early in January 1943 Fred's squadron was moved to the new satellite squadron at Fiskerton. At this time 617 Squadron was being formed at Scampton. We now know them as the *Dam Busters*. After 12 weeks we were posted to West Freugh, and Stranraer, in Scotland, on an air gunnery course; this time we flew in Ansons – slightly bigger planes. I was there six weeks altogether; We did a lot of flying but I spent most of my time on my wireless set, while the gunners were getting used to firing at target drogues and fighter aircraft taking part in fighter attacks.

Although I was training to be a gunner, it was all done on the ground. We fired the four Browning machine guns from a turret fixed to the ground. The target was a wooden plane going round in a circle on a cable. In the classroom we had to take the guns apart and put them back again, and just to make it easier we had to do it in the dark as well! – In all my RAF service I was never in a turret while in the air – and I never fired a gun while flying.

Fred did his last trip on the March 23rd 1943, and was awarded the DFC. He married Edna the next day – 24th March. He had completed 59 trips in all – quite an achievement. 'Let's hope I can do half as well as him,' I thought.

I did not go to the wedding as I was up in Scotland, in the middle of a course. (At this time Fred was stationed at Cranwell, and from there he had to go down to Buckingham Palace to receive his DFC.) We did a lot of strange things on this course. For example, we were put in an oxygen chamber, they then removed the oxygen, and we all passed out without knowing it. Before this happened we had been told to write our names and addresses on a board. A few minutes later we were told to look at our boards. Our addresses were only half complete – the pencil marks ran right down the board. Now I knew what it was like for a pilot when he passed out in a steep dive (G force).

One Anson pilot we flew with was a bit of a dare-devil; he used to fly low over the water and then dip his wing until it almost touched it. Accidents sometimes sprang from this sort of thing and crews were killed unnecessarily. At this stage I would like to ask readers to excuse me for switching so frequently between my own experiences and stories about brother Fred.

During his next job Fred was signals leader in charge of several flights of aircrew. Although my brother had a lot of near misses – fighter attack; flak; bombing of the squadron; several airmen killed – he still came out of it in one piece.

After some leave I was posted to Lossiemouth in Scotland. It wasn't an easy place to get to. We travelled by train; I got as far as Aberdeen at 8 p.m. and there wasn't a train until 6 o'clock on the following morning. I had to sleep in the waiting room.

Lossiemouth was to be our operational training unit (OTU) and we were flying Wellingtons. My pal, Leslie Kilpatrick, was now in the RAF under training as aircrew, I saw him when I was on leave, he was feeling pretty happy with himself; he was following my footsteps, not as a Wop/Ag, but as a signaller, wearing an 'S' badge. After two years' training I received my Wop/Ag brevet and sergeant's tapes. Everyone in the barracks was busy stitching them on their uniforms. The atmosphere was terrific; it was a proud moment for all of us.

Later, all of us met in a large room for a pep talk by one of the officers. His last words were: 'you are the cream of the cream'. I expect all the squads got the same talk; how can anyone express his feelings at such moments?

An OTU was where aircrew got together to form seven-men crews – to form a team – and you selected your own crew members. Imagine a large room full of sprog (new recruit) aircrew getting to know each other – Canadians, Australians, New Zealanders, South Africans, and of course English – and a lot of Scotsmen.

Each crew needed a pilot, navigator, bomb-aimer, engineer, wireless operator, and two gunners – mid-upper and rear. Three Canadians joined together (pilot, nav, and bomb-aimer) and they were looking for a wop. They came over to me and said: would you like to join us? They did not have much of a choice – I think I was the last one left. I was 5ft 3in tall and looked nearer to 16 than my 21 years. We didn't get our engineer and two gunners until later on; two of them were only 18 years old and the other 19.

My pilot's name was Van Slyke – a Dutch-Canadian. He towered over me. The navigator, another Canadian, was the only officer in the crew. His name was McGillavary. The bomb-aimer McDonagh, was a French-Canadian, while the engineer, Whitelaw, was a Scotsman. Then there was myself, Ball, Wop/Ag (the only Englishman); The mid-upper gunner, Grant (Scotsman); and the rear gunner, Collingwood (Scotsman). I was the 'referee' between these two. We did a lot of flying in Wellingtons, mock bombing of London when the Germans were quiet, and this was the first time we had flown as a crew in Wellingtons. We practised plenty of take off and landings – quite a lot to Elgin, a few miles away. Also we had 'fighter affiliation' to give the gunners a bit of practice. Almost all the time I was flying I was busy with my Marconi set, getting in touch with ground stations all over Scotland; we certainly kept the ground wops busy.

It wasn't until later on that we found out that Grant lived in Elgin. It is funny he never invited the crew to his home.

We nearly got blown up once when a photo-flash got stuck in the chute. These were used to light up the target; Their explosion was equivalent to a 250 lb bomb going off. But for the quick action of one of the crew, who put his hand down the chute and forced the flash through, I might not be alive today.

Even during training there was always the risk of accidents. Another shock: on one flight we were struck by lightning; we lost our trailing aerial, a flash in my set, also in the generator which was in the starboard engine and supplied all the power to the aircraft.

Back to the crew. Straight away we got on well together: no-one else existed except us seven – after all, our lives depended on one another. Most of our spare time was spent gambling, in the sergeants' mess or even in our billets. The most popular games were blackjack and shoot pontoon – a game you can win or lose in a very short space of time.

The night before we were posted from Lossiemouth we played cards. I won £22 in about ten minutes. We left the next day on leave so the lads never got a chance to win their money back. This win of mine was a lot of money in those days. My pay was 13 shillings and 6 pence per day. The commonwealth aircrew all had a lot more money than we did; some were real hard cases at gambling. The game with dice, 'crap,' used to be very popular.

Back home on leave in Harrogate the town was full of servicemen and women. Most of the hotels had been taken over by the airforce – airmen and WAAFs. Droves of aircrew who had come straight from Canada and America came to Harrogate, which was a transit camp.

Mum and dad had now been separated for quite a while. Dad had a flat two streets away from our house.

Sister Marjorie was seeing a sergeant navigator who was stationed at Dishforth. He flew in Whitley bombers; when he came home on leave at the same time as me we played cards a lot, but he was a bad loser.

Marjorie used to get mad with us, as she did not see much of him when he was at home. His name was Denny and he was a

Londoner. He had already done several trips over Germany. He was fed up with flying so he went to his commanding officer and refused to fly anymore. To me that took more courage than the actual flying. His tapes were taken away from him and 'LMF' (lack of moral fibre) was marked on his records. I don't know how things turned out for him but I felt sorry. After my leave I was posted to Marston Moor – a conversion unit – and there we were flying Halifaxes, four-engine bombers with triangular fins.

Group Captain Cheshire, who later got the VC for his exploits with the Dam Busters, and at that time was flying Lancasters, also flew Halifaxes at Marston Moor. Years later, I went to Canada and saw my bomb-aimer, McDonah. He told me a weird tale of how I tipped up Cheshire. Apparently, four of us were sitting on a form getting a bit of practice at morse sending. Cheshire was at one end and I was at the other. Two airmen got up from the centre and walked away. A few minutes later I got up and the form tipped, throwing Cheshire on the floor. McDonagh said I looked scared and stood to attention. You would think I would have remembered a situation like that.

We did a lot of flying in the new aircraft, day and night. My job was much the same whatever aircraft we were in – getting in touch with as many stations as possible all round the country.

The pilot and engineer had the hardest task; it was a big jump from Wellingtons to Halifaxes. The engineer had four engines to look after instead of two. On ops there was very little fuel to spare, so he had to have complete control of the flow of petrol to the engines. Each trip we did I had to make out a log for the signals officer, so we had to keep on our toes.

Most squadrons had their share of accidents – some fatal – and we were no exception. An example: three aircraft left Marston Moor for Snaith a few miles away, to practise circuits and bumps, (take offs and landings); the first Halifax landed in a gun pit at the side of the runway, and we landed perfectly on the runway. When the third Halifax landed, its brakes must have failed because the aeroplane went straight into the back of us. Collingwood, the rear gunner, saw the blades coming towards him, ripping the tailplane at each side of him, but they never touched the turret. We stayed the night at Snaith, and went back to Marston Moor by truck.

When we got any leave I used to take the crew home to Harrogate. One of our favourite pubs was The Exchange – rather a low dive – which was always crowded, so to save time we used to fill the table with about a dozen bottles of Bass ale and stay there till turning out time. There was dancing all night. Some of the French-Canadians did a lot of damage there, including throwing chairs through windows. Later they were barred.

About this time a lot of new equipment came into use on the camp. Besides 'GEE radar', which we had been taught at Cranwell, one of the new ones was 'Monica'. If, when you were flying and another plane approached (enemy or not) you would get a signal; the nearer the aircraft the louder it was. 'Mandrel' and 'Obo' also came into use. 'Fido' was a runway made out of burning petrol.

It saved the lives of a lot of crews who would not otherwise have been able to see in the fog. Back to the crew. I should have mentioned it before – our engineer, Whitelaw, was a smashing pianist and everywhere we went he was the centre of attraction. Whether in a pub or in the sergeants' mess, we used to sit and watch him play all night; my favourite was 'Boogy Woogy' and 'Stagecoach' played at the same time. It was the craze in 1943.

At Marston Moor we did not have a lot of spare time. We were kept busy; A few more weeks and we would be going to our squadron, and then the fun would start.

5

158 Squadron, Lissett

December, 1943: we finished our conversion and were posted to our squadron, 158, Lissett, four miles from Bridlington. I was a sergeant, Wop, ready for ops after almost two years' training. That training had taken me from Cardington to Blackpool, Yatesbury, Feltwell, Mildenhall, Yatesbury again, West Freugh, Stranraer, Lossiemouth, Elgin, Manby, Marston Moor, and now Lissett. Now that training was all over – or so we thought – a new, more powerful, Halifax had come off the assembly lines – the Mark III. This had square tailplanes, so as soon as we arrived on the squadron our training started all over again, to get used to the new aircraft.

When I think back, at least we were postponing our possible demise a little longer, as at this time a lot of aircraft were being lost. When we first entered the sergeants' mess, a group of aircrew were discussing what was in a newspaper. We found out later that one of the rear gunners had been taking a torch with him on ops; he was shining it out of his turret to attract enemy fighters. Although I think he shot down one or two fighters he was taking an awful risk with the rest of his crew, as well as disobeying orders. On night bombing raids our job was to get to our target as soon as possible, drop our bombs, and avoid all enemy action, if possible. If you were attacked by fighters you had no choice but to defend yourself.

When we were not playing cards in the mess, the crew used to go to Bridlington. We got to know a group of WAAFs who were billeted out at one of the private hotels on the promenade. We spent a lot of time there; they had a piano and Whitelaw was in his element. We used to sing all the latest songs; one of the girls had a good singing voice; I remember once I was sitting in a chair listening to the music when Joan came over and sat on my lap and started to sing, 'There's a gold mine in the sky far away'. We spent many happy hours there.

Van Slyke's crew got to be well known, even by the WAAF orderly sergeant who used to check all the billets to see that every visitor had left by ten o'clock; she used to shine her torch on us and say: 'oh, Van Slyke's crew here again', and then walk out.

At the end of 1943 Fred was at Halfpenny Green (an advanced flying unit near Wolverhampton) as a signals leader, flying Ansons as an instructor. He was moved about a lot to different stations. Although he had finished his ops, there was still a certain amount of danger as he was still flying, and a lot of accidents were happening during training. The Pavilion dance hall and picture house in Bridlington was taken over by the RAF; the lower part was used as a cookhouse, and the rest for trainee engineers, aircrew; the corporal WAAF who was a friend of ours was in charge. One night we left it too late to get back to camp, so we slept between the seats in the theatre, all seven of us. Next morning the WAAFs came round at about 6 o'clock and asked us what we wanted for breakfast. We went into the kitchen where rows of trays were laid out with bacon and kidneys. We were told to help ourselves; we had a good thing going, the WAAFs were so friendly. Joan, the one with the voice, went out with Collingwood our rear gunner, and I was a friend of Jacky, the corporal, who was in charge of the billet. As far as I knew it was all platonic friendship. Later on Joan went out with McGillivary, the only officer in the crew, and that started a lot of bad feelings, not with the crew but with the WAAFs themselves who thought she had played a dirty trick.

About this time McGillivary had to go into hospital with yellow jaundice so we had to look around for a spare navigator. Usually when a crew had any trouble and someone got killed, they split up the crew who then became 'spares' – a spare could also be someone who'd been posted to the squadron on his own.

All the Commonwealth crews were waiting in the mess to see

if there were any ops on that night, 20th January 1944. The mess was like a gambling joint; almost everyone was playing cards of some sort round the tables; nobody took any notice of the signs round the walls saying 'no gambling in the mess'. At least it took our minds off the matter in hand.

An officer walked in and said, 'ops on tonight.' He made no mention of the target, though. It was a funny feeling you got; I cannot explain it, not fear or panic – just apprehension. This was our *baptism of fire*.

Most of the trips took off at about eight o'clock at night. At last orders came through and we had to report to the briefing room. When everyone had sat down and there was quiet, a cover was taken off the notice board, showing a map of Germany. The target was Berlin, the worst of the lot. We received our briefing from the signals leader, Sandy Sandall, and went to our new aircraft Halifax, H, Mark III.

All the crew got aboard; everyone was excited. Our first trip! What was it going to be like? What we should have been thinking was 'will we be coming back?'

As it happened we had to return with engine trouble; we had been flying for about 50 minutes when first one and then another engine packed up. We had no choice but to dump our bombs and return to base. That was a nice start to our tour. When you had to return like this it made you feel guilty, although it happened to most crews at some time or another. 158 Squadron lost one crew and two aircraft had to return to base on this occasion.

It must have been awful for my mother. After going through Fred's tours (59 trips) she had to start all over again with me. It was worst for Fred's wife, Edna, because she lived in Lincoln, and most of the Lancasters flew over her house, when a raid was on.

Next night, 21 January 1944, we were on ops again. Little did we know what was in front of us this time. The target was Magdeburg, about 80 miles from Berlin. As our navigator, McGillivary was still in hospital, we took a 'spare' nav with us this time, Evans. He had already done two trips, and this one was going to be his last.

This time we got to our target, dropped our bombs and got away as soon as we could. The bomb-aimer said we were dead on. When bombs were dropped a photo was taken – hence the use of the photo-flash. We did not have time to think about danger or anything like that. I was busy all the time dropping 'window', – metal strips which interrupted the German long range high frequency direction finding (HFDF). We were also given a frequency from No. 4 group HQ of the German fighter SRDF, and we were jamming it; at the beginning of the war you had to keep radio silence and listen out only.

In my position in the plane I had a small window with a curtain. I moved it to one side and saw the target – a mass of flames as far as the eye could see. There was puffs of black smoke all around us which were exploding shells.

We got away from the target area and were on our way back to base, when the trouble started. We were running out of petrol, the engineer did his best to control the rate of flow from the petrol tanks to save as much as possible. Our spare nav said his GEE radar had packed up on him, and the next time I saw him he was at the rear escape hatch.

It was no use. Two of the engines had packed up and we were going down. Van Slyke, the pilot, shouted over the intercom warning us to get ready to ditch in the sea, although we could not have been far from the English coast. The pilot asked me to send out an SOS signal, which I did, and try to get in touch with base to get a 'QDM', a course to steer.

The rear gunner and navigator were already at the rear of the aircraft when the bomb-aimer, who was in the front position, shouted that he could see the waves down below, so the pilot gave orders to bale out. Our squadron was based four miles from Bridlington. In the meantime, I was still working on my set. I was in touch with base and received a third class bearing from Lissett and Driffield. I had another go and this time I got a second class bearing: this is what I was trained for. Thank goodness I was able to complete my job – what was on my mind all the time was that I might let the crew down.

We must have been well below 1500 ft and going down fast; I disconnected my intercom and put my chute on with difficulty. I went down to the rear of the aircraft and saw the hatch was open. Collingwood, the rear gunner, and Evans, the navigator, were already sitting on the edge of the opening. We will never know why they were waiting there; maybe they had disconnected their intercom and did not hear the order to bale out; anyway, it cost them their lives.

I went straight to the opening and rolled out into blackness. I felt a tug and then I hit a hedge and landed in a ploughed field. There were only seconds between life and death.

The next two to bale out hit the ground before their chutes opened. It must have been a quick death; they wouldn't have felt a thing.

It was always said that a jump at under 1000 ft was a suicide jump; we must have been at about 500 ft when I jumped. It was different if you had a cord attached to your chute like a paratrooper.

Grant, the mid-upper gunner, and the engineer had already baled out and were alright. The pilot and bomb-aimer stayed and went down with the aircraft, and as the RAF records show, pulled off a magnificent 'wheels down' forced landing in a field not far from the squadron base.

Although Lissett and Driffield had been contacted, and they had sent up rockets to guide us in, we did not see them. I picked up my chute and walked back to camp about a quarter of a mile away.

When I got back, crowds of aircrew who had already got back safely were waiting for us; they had heard the noise of our engines but could not see us. It was a very dark night. Sandy Sandall, the signals officer, came over to me and said, the section had been praying for us, and 'good show, you did a good job'. This had been our baptism of fire. Two killed. Collingwood was only 18 years old. I never saw the bodies but McDonagh did; they looked as if they were asleep on the ground, with blood trickling from their eyes, nose and ears.

I was now a member of the Caterpillar Club for saving my life by parachute. When I first got back to camp I did not know what had happened to the rest of the crew; I sat on a chair in one of the huts in a sort of daze. Shock, I suppose.

We learned later that we had lost 53 aircraft that night: that is 371 aircrew lost, probably two-thirds of them killed, and the rest wounded, and taken prisoner.

After all the excitement had died down we were sent on survivors' leave. Van, the pilot, and McGillivary the navigator, being Canadians, just stayed at our house for a few days, then went off sightseeing, probably to pick up some girls. McDonagh went down to London by himself.

Leslie, my best pal, was also on leave and staying at my house as usual. He was now a sergeant/signaller and wore an 'S' brevet instead of Wop/Ag. He was stationed at my old OTU, Lossiemouth. We did feel proud walking around the town together, even though Harrogate was still packed with aircrew. We were now real 'Brylcream Boys' as the other services called us.

I got a nice surprise when I went to the central cinema in Harrogate. The Pathe Gazette News showed a big raid on Magdeburg. The full target area was in front of me, just as I saw it when I was over the target – a mass of flames and explosions. It seemed like a dream; I must have been more tired than I realised because I fell asleep. I'd never done that before in a cinema.

In the meantime, McDonagh ran out of money in London and went back to the squadron base. A few weeks later we found out he had been on two more trips with another crew – Leipzig, February 19, and Stuttgart, February 20, when the squadron lost two planes (one by fighter, the other crashed). Just like McDonagh – he would volunteer for anything.

At this time Wing Commander Calder was flying with 158 Squadron; later, he went on to Lancasters; he was the first pilot to drop the 22,000 lb bomb, the biggest of the war.

When we came off leave, that same night we went to Bridlington and called round at the WAAF's billet. We were told Joan had been crying her eyes out over Collingwood when she heard he had been killed. She had, after all, played a dirty trick on him by going out with McGillivary. She was only young; maybe it was the uniform. After a few days it was all forgotten, outwardly anyway.

As we were minus a rear gunner the pilot had to choose one from the spares. We were lucky; one was available who had already done one tour – a chap named Mardon Mowbray. His wife was expecting a baby, and they lived in York. By now our own navigator had come out of hospital, and was fit to fly. There was one difficulty: the wing commander had decided to split our crew up; this was usual when you had casualties, so we did the only thing we could do – McDonagh and I went to see the commanding officer and told him that if he split us up we wouldn't fly again. He could have stripped us to the ranks, but instead he said that seeing as we felt that way we could keep together. It would have been unthinkable, flying with a strange crew because now we were close together.

On February 24 we took part in a raid on Schweinfurt ball-bearing factories. Our squadron lost no aircraft but Wing Commander Calder's crew saw 12 aircraft go down on the run to the target. On February 25th we went to Augsburg; again we did not lose any aircraft, but a lot of aerial combat took place between Augsburg and Stuttgart.

March 1 we went to Stuttgart – no aircraft lost. March 6 we went to Trappes in France – no aircraft lost. March 7 we went to Le Mans in France – no aircraft lost. March 13 Le Mans again – no aircraft lost. We came back from two of these trips without brakes and ran off the runway into a ploughed field; no one was hurt; there was just slight damage to the plane. We also landed with a 1000 lb bomb we had been unable to release.

On one of the trips a message came over on my set in code saying: 'enemy fighters on your track, change course'. It was a long message; I missed about three letters – but we still understood it. We found out later it was a hoax; maybe it was sent to see if the wireless ops were doing their job and were alert; we still had to make a log out on every trip. All the time we were not on ops we were still training, fighter affiliation, cross-country runs, air-to-air firing, night fighter aff., bomb load take-offs; we had no time to think of danger.

On March 15th we went to Stuttgart. 831 bombers were sent, and 36 crews were lost; most of these raids involved up to a thousand planes; 158 Squadron did not lose any. During our training we went on outings to see how the other half lived. Some were sent round a chocolate factory in York; the group I was in went down a coal mine, at Micklefield in Yorkshire. They took us down in a lift then we travelled for some distance by train; when we got to where the miners were working we were told to take cover, and they started blasting. I don't know whether it had all been arranged for us but it came as a bit of a shock.

About this time we had a rest period and the crews were sent on a battle course with the army. All the RAF officers and NCOs wore denims, and we took our orders from the army; we were there about a week; cross country runs, unarmed combat, and gunnery were the call of the day.

One night – it was about midnight, and pouring with rain –

they gave us a rifle and we had to black our faces. They said: 'now we have a job for you to do; we want you to attack a machine gun emplacement a few miles away without being seen'. We had to crawl along the ground in all the rain, what a mess we were in when we got back to camp.

Back at 158 Squadron base, we were playing cards in the mess for a change when a sergeant walked in. I recognised him straight away; he had lived next door to me at Chapel Court in Harrogate; we had a long talk about old times. His name was Louie Craven; it must have been about ten years since I had last seen him. As it happened we were all on ops that night and he never returned. At the time I thought he had been killed, but that was not so; I saw his sister years later, and she told me a different story. Louie was stationed at Driffield, but quite often they took off from Lissett then returned to their home base, and he was alright on that night. Louie actually copped it later, the same week as I did – me on the 24th March 1944, and him on the big Nuremburg raid on 30 March, when over 90 aircraft failed to return. This was the most lost in any one night. In those days you were lucky to survive more than a few weeks.

On March 18th we went to Frankfurt, one of the tougher targets; 158 Squadron lost one aircraft to fighter attack. On March 23rd we attacked Frankfurt again; we lost two, shot down by fighters. While over Frankfurt, a queer thing happened to us; we were coned by a group of searchlights; all of a sudden they parted, leaving us a long passage to fly through. We thought this was it – enemy fighters would be waiting for us at the end of it. But no, we got clear; we had a guardian angel that night. When you got caught in searchlights the usual thing was to go into a dive.

March 24th 1944. This proved to be our last trip: the 'Big City', Berlin. It was a bad day for us. Whitelaw had invited all the crew to Edinburgh to his wedding; he had hired a hall. It was going to be a big affair; his parents had a big haulage firm in Edinburgh.

Mowbray had a wife living in York; her baby was now due at any time. It was bad for people you left behind; they probably suffered more than we did, not knowing what was happening to us. We had a job to do and knew what to expect.

This should have been told earlier in the story. I mention it now to show you how dedicated the crews were towards each other. We had been into battle and proved ourselves; it was then that

my skipper, Van, told me that when he'd first seen me in Lossiemouth, he had not thought much of me at all. After Magdeburg he
was like a father to me; he used to call me son. The idea of splitting
the crew up was completely wrong.

One night when we were in a Bridlington pub – all the crew of
course – having a quiet drink together, an officer came over to us
and said, 'are you Van Slyke's crew'. When we answered, 'yes,'
he asked if he could join us. We did not know his name but he
was the adjutant of 158 Squadron. He said: 'your crew have been
making a name for yourselves; you are the talk of the camp with
all the bad luck you have been having; now that you have done
quite a few trips you should settle down and finish your tour.' A
week later we were on the missing list.

Back to Berlin. The trip to the target area was uneventful, but
as we were making our run in, we were attacked by a Junkers 88
– the new version which fired cannon shells from a gun on the
nose. It came from underneath. The German pilot had the advantage; we were not protected when the attack was from this quarter.

The bomb-aimer had just released our bombs and was laid flat
in the nose of the aircraft, so he got the full blast of the cannonsh-
ells all down his side, leg and foot. Two engines were set on fire,
then the Junkers 88 came in again, and gave the bomb-aimer
another dose. By this time the plane was out of control and going
into a spin. Of the 810 aircraft on that raid, 73 were lost. A few
days later at Nuremberg (30th March 1944) 90 aircraft were lost;
well over 1000 aircrew were killed or taken prisoner in one week.

Bomber Command losses were greater than any other service
in the war. The raid on Berlin was the last raid on that target in
which 1000 bombers took part.

McDonagh was taken to a Berlin hospital; he was in a bad way.
The German doctor told him he had 48 pieces of metal in him. I
was still working on my set when the curtain which separated me
from the nose of the aircraft blew in; I could hear the thud, thud
of the cannon shells hitting us; putting my head round the corner,
flames were all over the place. The navigator had blood on his
forehead; still on the intercom I heard the skipper say, 'for Christ
sake get out of this aircraft'.

Under these conditions the plane could explode at any time; it
was every man for himself. Putting my parachute on was no easy
job; it was to my right, strapped to the framework. I got hold of

it and tried to put it on my harness, but it went up to the roof. It took all my strength to fix it on. As I was leaving I heard the rear gunner screaming, 'I can't get out of my turret'. With the plane going into a spin no way could I have got to the rear to help him out, when I think back I must be the only one alive that heard him screaming.

Grant, the mid-upper, and McGillivary the navigator had already baled out. The usual way of getting out of a turret was to turn round and fall out backwards, but if the hydraulics didn't work, and the manual control was not working, you were stuck. It is possible that he was hit with cannon shells.

The front escape hatch was already open. I saw someone on the edge, but things were so hectic I can't remember who it was – more than likely the bomb-aimer. He must have been in a lot of pain; of course I didn't know his predicament until I met him in the POW camp in East Prussia weeks later. I could hear the noise of the slipstream as I jumped out into space. We had been flying at about 21,000 ft when attached, and freezing level was 1000 ft I mention this because I left my gloves in the plane. I usually took them off when I was dropping down the chute.

When my chute opened, I could see all the earth below me on fire. I knew that if I landed in that then if the fires didn't finish me off the civilians would. A dome like that of St Paul's Cathedral was silhouetted against the skyline. Later, when I was in East Prussia, I saw a picture of it in a German magazine. As there was strong winds that night, I drifted away from the target into blackness.

At the time I had no idea where I was or where I would land. It was so cold. You needed oxygen at anything over 10,000 ft. There was always the risk of your passing out. Without thinking I put one hand inside my battle dress, and the other inside the flyhole of my trousers; this probably saved me from frostbite. I made a nice soft landing in the middle of a dyke; the March winds were strong that night; I was pulled along by my chute for quite a distance before I could release myself. With the soaking I got I must have looked like a drowned rat, in the end that is how I was when the Germans caught me.

Almost every crewman who got shot down and survived had a story to tell. We have heard from German pilots after the war that the land below the run in to the target was littered with British bombers, and in 1944 the new Junkers 88 took a terrible toll with their cannon shells.

Here is a story which coincides with my own experience. This chap was a Wop/Ag stationed at Lissett. He flew Halifaxes and lost three of his crew, the only difference being that he was shot down in August 1943, and I in March 1944. He tells a better story than I ever could:

'Baling out of a blazing bomber over Berlin, one of the most heavily defended cities in Germany, could possibly be described as baling out of hell into hell, as I experienced at midnight on 31 August 1943, when a Halifax bomber of 158 Squadron, Lissett, in which I was flying as a wireless operator/air gunner, was attacked directly over the target by enemy night fighters seconds after the bombs were dropped, and immediately the bomb doors closed. Seconds earlier and the whole crew would have perished instead of only three.

No evasive action can possibly be carried out on a bombing run. To bale out of a blazing bomber, still under attack, with two engines on fire, and completely out of control, coned by searchlights, amongst 600 bombers dropping bombs from various heights, night fighters, flares, and bursting shells from anti-aircraft guns, gave thoughts to the extreme danger when the parachute opened and gently drifted away from the nightmare of the target. Thoughts, in the dark and dangerous sky, of the fate of the rest of the crew. How many had been killed in this hell? You look around in the sky for parachutes. You see nothing. The searchlights sweep the sky as if looking for you, assisting the night fighters in their attack.

You watch with fascination the blazing target, the explosions of the bombs, and the retaliation of the anti-aircraft guns, with little thought of the thousands of tons of flak in the air.

You wonder if the tracer bullets you see are coming from an air gunner's turret, or from an enemy fighter attacking another bomber. You watch with dismay a blazing bomber plunging down to earth, and wonder if anyone got out.

Your parachute seems to be going up, instead of coming down, and you feel slightly sick with the swaying. You begin to wonder what height you are when you see a night fighter only a little way above you; and how long . . . and where will you hit the ground? Will you be shot when you are in the hands of the enemy? Or shown mercy as a POW? All these thoughts, as you slowly, alone, and completely helpless, descend into the unknown. Your face feels wet with perspiration – or is it raining? You feel a little numb in this dark, unreal world and wonder if you are dreaming. The crunch of an anti-aircraft shell nearby reminds you that you are not, as the bombing continues.

You listen to the humming engines of the bombers. Some will be shot down on the way home, perhaps over the sea. All the way back to the English coast – and sometimes inland – they will be pursued by determined enemy night fighters, with their excellent radar, and equally brave pilots eager to be credited with the destruction of another bomber. The bomber crews are alert to all this, and do not relax for one moment.

As you are mesmerised by the red glow in the sky from the fires, observing the flashes from the anti-aircraft guns, and the shellbursts in the sky, you begin to think of your loved ones at home. In a few hours they will receive that dreaded telegram, which they have been expecting ever since you started operational flying – 'Regret to inform you that your . . .' (I still have mine), and you begin to think: 'will I ever see them again?'

I hope to meet him one of these days.

Later on I heard that three bodies had been found in a burnt out Halifax: Van Slyke the pilot, Whitelaw the engineer and Mowbray the rear gunner, had gone down with the plane. Was it possible the pilot was badly wounded, or that he stayed at the controls to give the rear gunner a better chance of getting out of his turret, and left it too late? Once a plane goes down in a spin it is difficult to get out, and I should know.

Grant, the other gunner, was burnt slightly on the neck from the fires coming from the engines when he baled out. McGillivary the navigator only had a scratch on his forehead.

McDonagh had it the worst. When McGillivary finally found him he was off his head; he said a German soldier had found him and hit him over the head with a rifle butt, and he was muttering all sorts of things. McGillivary stayed with him until they were captured. He gave up his chance of escape; he had no choice; he had to help him; crews stuck together.

McDonagh was taken to a German hospital where the doctor

said he had all those pieces of metal in him. He was wounded all down his right side; his flying boot was ripped to pieces. Within a very short time he went from 11 st. down to 6 st.

Back home my parents received the usual letter from our commanding officer offering the squadron's condolences, and declaring that I had been reported missing, believed killed, over Berlin.

In the same week my best pal Leslie Kilpatrick was killed at Lossiemouth. The news I got was ('not confirmed') that his plane crashed into the sea after take off and his body was never found.

About that time the powers that be allowed OTUs and conversion crews to make up the numbers on 1000 bomber raids. Anyway, he was reported: 'killed in action'. Both our photographs were in the Harrogate papers; he was 19 and I 22.

Brother Fred and his wife came home on leave to celebrate their anniversary – March 24th 1944. He could see mother didn't look so good so he asked her what was the matter. 'Harry did not return from a raid last night', she said. My family never showed much emotion but that does not mean anything; they kept their feelings to themselves.

It was three months later, in June, when a telegram arrived to say I was a prisoner of war in German hands. After all that time they must have given me up for dead. By this time my sister, Marjorie, had met a Canadian engine fitter who she was very fond of, and eventually married.

Letter from my commanding officer to my mother and letters to my mother from the mothers of crew members.

1583/C.452/89/PI.   No. 158 Squadron,
                                    ROYAL AIR FORCE.
                                    25th March, 1944.

Dear Mrs Ball,

It is with the greatest regret that I have to write confirming the news given in my telegram of today that your son, Sgt Harry

Ball has been reported missing from an operational sortie against Berlin on the night of 24/25th March, 1944.

The aircraft in which your son was Wireless Operator took off at 18.50 hrs on 24th March, since then nothing has been heard. There is, of course, a possibility that the crew may have landed safely, but it is too early to expect any news of such an eventuality. Should I hear anything I will communicate with you immediately.

It is desired to explain that the request in the telegram notifying you of the casualty was included with the object of avoiding his chance of escape being prejudiced by undue publicity in case he was still at large. This is not to say that any information about him is available, but is a precaution adopted in the case of all personnel reported missing. I am enclosing a list of the names and addresses of the next of kin of the rest of the crew, in case you want to communicate with them. Your son's personal effects are being collected and will be sent to the Standing Committee of Adjustment, Colnbrook, Slough for onward transmission to you in due course.

If you should wish to make any enquiry regarding your son's effects, will you please address it to the Effects Officer, RAF Station, Driffield, East Yorkshire.

May I, on behalf of myself and the Squadron as a whole, extend to you our sincere sympathy and understanding at this anxious time.

Yours Sincerely,

Wing Commander, Commanding,
No. 158 Squadron, R.A.F.

Mrs A. Ball,   Central Butte,
18 Mount Parade,   Saskatchewan, Canada.
Harrogate,   June 18th, 1944.
Yorkshire.

My navigator's mother.

Dear Mrs Ball,

We are happy to tell you that Allan is a Prisoner of War. We do
hope you have had the same good news of your son, we know
things won't be so pleasant for them, but at least they are
alright, and the (Red Cross) are so good about providing food
and clothing for them.

We have had a letter from Mrs McDonagh saying Norman is
a prisoner too, so we feel sure the rest of the crew are alright.

The war is really going ahead lately, and surely old Hitler will
see the trap approaching, it will be a happy day when it is all
over.

Hoping to hear good news from you soon,

I am yours sincerely,

Mrs McGillivary.

                                               Red Deer,
                                         Alberta Canada,
                                               July 1944,
The mother of the pilot, Van Slyke.

Dear Mrs Ball and Marjorie,

I am writing this note to both of you at once. Hope you will
excuse me, got your lovely letters and thanks so much for them.
It does seem nice to hear from the people who knew Allan, we
seem to have so much in common, as Harry and Allan are the
only two not heard from.

Time seems so long – over four months since that fatal trip; surely if they had lost their lives they would have been found and reported long before this. They may be in hiding somewhere, we can still hope and pray.

We are so thankful to know that four out of the seven are prisoners. Some day they will be home and can tell us of that perilous trip. Mrs Grant, (Mid-Upper Gunner's Mother), tells me they had a hard trip in Jan; the crew bailed out when they reached the English coast, Allan never told us anything, only they got along OK.

Allan's girl (Winnie Curan) wrote and said that (Kenneth Marsdon Mowbray) is presumed dead. I had a letter from his wife, but he was still missing when she wrote, she is expecting a wee one in September, poor dear girl, she sent me a little picture of them both.

Thanks so much for (Harry's picture), it is lovely, and we know which one is Harry, we have such a nice picture of just he and Allan.

I also had a nice letter from Mrs Whitelaw (Engineer) and Mrs Grant, also Mrs McGillivary, they spoke so nicely of Allan.

I do hope Marjorie you are happily married, and that you will come to Canada after this cruel war is over. I surely wish Allan could bring Harry back with him, as he did like him so much, also hope your other brother is fine.

Our son Donald was in the hospital in Italy with an abscess on his hip. He said he read a book each day, so he wasn't very sick, he does write cheerful letters. Now Mrs Ball, this will be all for tonight, will have to keep in touch.

We will have to keep smiling for the rest of the family, and hope and pray for our lads who are away.

Yours most Truly,

Addie Van Slyke,

This last letter was sent after my parents had received word that I was a POW.

Central Butte,
Saskatchewan,
Canada,
Aug 20th, 1944.

Dear Mrs Ball,

I was so glad to hear your son was a prisoner of war. While it may not be so pleasant, it is a wonderful feeling to know that they are alive and well. We have had a few letters from Allan, of course they can say very little, but it is nice to receive word in their own writing.

We are still waiting to hear from Mrs Van Slyke, they have had no official word of their son yet, it is hard to have to wait so long. We hope they will soon be home now, and then they will be able to tell us all about it. It is two years since Allan was last home, the time does get very long. The war is really getting ahead now, surely the Germans won't be able to last out much longer.

We are very busy with the harvest now, the cutting of wheat is in full swing now, the crops are lovely this year.

The girls were all home the first two weeks in July, but we just have three home now, Gladys the married girl stays with us, her husband is in England with the RCAF, I believe he is stationed not far from where you live, it isn't far from Hull.

The other girls at home are twelve and eight years. Norma is in the RCAF. Alice teaches school, and Irene keeps books for a store. Allan is in Stalagluft 1, is that where your boy is?

Mrs McDonagh's boy is at Dulagluft, so the crew are widely separated. I received a letter from Mrs Mowbray. (Rear Gunner's Wife), saying her husband was believed killed. There are so many broken hearts, it does seem too bad such things have to be. I will be glad to hear from you frequently, we like to keep in touch with you.

Sincerely Yours,

Mrs John McGillivary.

It is amazing how long it took for the information to come through from the Red Cross – in our case three months. Even then most of the news was not up to date. In one letter it was said that the crew had separated from one another. This happened only in the case of McGillivary: because he was an officer he went to Stalagluft 1. The main officers' camp was Stalagluft 3, Sargon.) He stayed at No. 1 until the end of the war, when he was released.

McDonagh (after he came out of a Berlin Hospital), Grant and myself went to Stalagluft 6, Heydekrug, East Prussia.

Van Slyke, Mowbray and Whitelaw, went down with the plane; they were unable to get out. Although aircrew underwent a lot of stress, most of us did not feel it at the time. It was the wives and families who bore the blunt, not knowing what was happening to us.

6

Capture in Germany

When I pulled myself together I realised what a mess I was in. It was pitch black, I was on German soil, I had no idea where I was, and no idea where the rest of my crew were. I could still hear the drone of our aircraft going home; it was hard to believe I had been having egg and chips in the sergeants' mess a few hours earlier.

On burying my chute under the bank of the dyke I started to look for somewhere to sleep. Eventually I found a group of buildings and chose the largest. It turned out to be a barn. Inside the building the main supports were square, not round. When I climbed up into the loft luck was with me. There was plenty of straw about. After all the excitement, I fell asleep, not knowing what was in front of me the next morning.

All of a sudden a noise below me broke the silence – men's and women's voices speaking German. A man climbed up into the loft with a stick in his hand; he must have seen my flying boots in the straw, although with all the planes being shot down this sort of thing was to be expected, and there must have been regular searches for aircrew.

This man pointed to a whistle in my battle dress, which was used to attract attention if you had to ditch in the sea. I took it and gave it to him. He seemed pleased; he beckoned me to follow him down. Below me was a row of unfriendly faces. Most of the farmers had farm implements with them; walking past them was a pretty nerve-racking experience; they looked at me in amazement. I must have looked more like a boy cadet than a 'terror flieger'or 'luft gangster'. That is what the Germans called us. I was then taken to the local jail and given some raw sausage and two slices of black bread. At first I could not eat it. After a while when I began to feel hungry, I had a go. It was quite an experience, sitting there in a cell with the Germans taking a peep at me every so often through a hole in the door; they must have thought I was public enemy no. 1. And the guards continued to keep an eye on me through the little hole in the door: you see, I was such a dangerous prisoner. The next day a private car came for me. Two men dressed in long trench coats. They could have been police, or even the Gestapo. Nobody said a word to me.

I was picked up near Brandenburg. Just my luck, it was a 'State Farm' where all the workers met before setting out on their different jobs. The two Germans took me to Berlin and dropped me outside a large building. It looked similar to our air ministry except for the statues of eagles, German soldiers all over the place, and of course German flags with swastikas. I was in full flying kit. They took me to a large room with men and women behind them. A uniformed man told me to strip to my vest and pants. What they were looking for I don't know. Mind you, we did carry a stud and comb which we could use as a compass.

I felt as if I was in a peep show – it was more like a dream – and that I would soon wake up. 'Get yourself dressed', the officer said, and then we left. Guards then took me to the railway station where I met my navigator. The station was a lot like Kings Cross, except someone was shouting over the loud speakers, 'Achtung, Achtung'; even some soldiers passed by us shouting, 'Heil Hitler'.

From then on we did not know what to expect. The people were shaking their fists at us. You could not blame them really; Berlin was a pile of rubble. It was surprising they had a railway left working.

My navigator and I got on the train; the guards with us were Luftwaffe and they had their guns drawn all the time; if they had been army SS more than likely they would have handed us over to the civilians. From Berlin to Frankfurt we had to stand up all the time, with the people watching us.

We were then taken to the interrogation centre, where we

should have received an attaché case with a Red Cross parcel, shaving gear, tooth brush and comb in it; we got nothing like that.

Interrogation

The people were in a nasty mood, shaking their fists, etc. We had been on two night raids on Frankfurt and the Americans had been twice during the day. Again, the place was a pile of rubble. I must admit I was a bit scared walking through a town like that in flying kit. You could almost feel the hatred in the air; but we managed to keep out of trouble, and got to the centre. The guards put us in separate cells, a small room with a bed. There was also a blanket, which I did not need. We had hot radiators on all the time. The window was barred with shutters outside, and there was the usual hole in the door where they could keep an eye on me.

One of the guards came in with some swede soup and a slice of black bread. Later on we were given some funny-tasting coffee. I understand it was made out of acorns.

The next day I was taken to the interrogation room. The officer in charge asked me if I would like a cigarette. I told him no, I did not smoke. He then offered me a biscuit which I took and said, 'thanks'. Now, in perfect English, he said, 'I want you to answer a few questions; we know which squadron you are from; all we want you to do is confirm it'.

During our training we had been taught, if ever we got taken prisoner, to give only our number, rank and name. Expecting all these questions, I couldn't help smiling when he asked me. Of course, that made him mad; he said, 'I could take you out and have you shot; you have no identity discs with you, you could be a spy, all I want is for you to tell us what we already know'. 'Sorry,' I said, 'number, rank and name.' So this time he gave up and sent me back to my cell. On the way to the toilets I saw my mid-upper gunner, Grant; he seemed to be in good health; you had to ask the guards every time you wanted to go. Most nights there were air raids; just outside my window I could hear the self-propelled guns or rockets going off, six at a time.

Most of the meals were two slices of black bread, potato and swede soup. I don't think there was any meat in it; coffee came twice a day. Most of the time I spent walking up and down the room. Now I knew how an animal feels in a cage; it was always warm in the cell, but I was hungry all the time, and we had plenty of time to think about it.

For 11 days the officer came round to my cell asking me the same questions. He said, 'as soon as you have answered you can go to a POW camp for the rest of the war.' 'Sorry', I said, 'number, rank and name.' On the 12th day I was taken to the guard's office. Whether he did this on purpose I do not know. He left the office for a while; on his table was a pile of papers and I was able to read the top sheet upside down. All the information was there; 158 Squadron, A Flight.

When the officer came in again he asked me the same question. 'What was your squadron?'

I was beginning to sound like a parrot: 'sorry, number rank and name.'

That same day we moved out.

My navigator told me later that he had confirmed what the officer wanted to know. He had left it all this time to give any of the crew a chance to escape. At that time we did not know what had happened to the rest of the crew; we did not give any secrets away.

The Long Journey

Now started the worst part of our journey; we were taken to a railway station where we were herded into cattle trucks; the whole train was packed with POWs. The entrance of each truck had sliding doors leading to two sections with a passage in between. The sections were closed together with wire, like a cage. I wondered how many Jews and political prisoners had travelled in them and never returned.

There were about 20 POWs each side; there was no room to lie down; we were like sardines in a tin; we travelled five days and five nights like this. When the doors were closed all we could see was a slit of light high up one side; at night we moved into railway sidings because of the bombing.

There was very little food for us: just soup, bread, and coffee twice a day. When we stopped everyone got out to go to the toilet.

There was a trough in the centre of the truck but I never saw anybody using it; it would have been most embarrassing, besides the smell.

At one of the stops a German nurse pointed towards me and asked one of the chaps, in broken English, how old I was. I was 22 but even in the state I was in I looked about 16.

As we travelled along what little of the landscape we could see was forest and countryside. Maybe we were going all round the big towns to avoid the bombing.

Through Germany, Poland, and East Prussia we went; it seemed never-ending, stopping and starting, moving into sidings; it was like playing hide and seek with our bombers.

We had no room to lie down in the truck; we were crushed together.

One night I woke up to find the lower part of my body numb with the weight of one of the chaps lying across me; it was a nightmare. I felt like screaming. Everywhere was dark, apart from the light from the slit in the side of the truck, maybe I had a touch of claustrophobia.

The trucks were loaded with POWs who had been captured from all over Europe – all allied aircrews.

7

POW Camps

Heydekrug

From the train we were marched to a place called Heydekrug. On nearing the entrance to the camp, we saw crowds of POWs behind the wire. Someone shouted, 'hello Bally.' It was Taffy Gibbs,one of the chaps who was CTd (ceased training, failure) at Blackpool; he was a rear gunner.

The camp was out in the wilds, surrounded by forests; it was separated into different compounds. In the corners of each compound was a postern box on four wooden posts, where the guards had Mauser machine guns. Guards patrolled outside the camp with dogs. All around the perimeter inside, about five yards wide, were notice boards saying, anyone entering this zone would be shot without warning. So it looked as if they wanted to keep us.

The camp consisted of rows of huts, with about 70 men in each. About 3000 Commonwealth aircrew were in one section, and the other part was taken over by the Americans.

As the British compound was full we were put in with the Americans – at first in tents and later into huts. We slept in double and sometimes treble bunks. After settling down we had to get used to a routine. We were counted twice a day on the parade ground. First thing in the morning, a lot of the chaps stayed in their night clothes with their great coats on top; this was alright as long as the commandant didn't see them; otherwise it was the cooler or solitary confinement.

At one time all POWs got one food parcel every week, but because of the bombing they were slow in coming through; at one time we had to share one parcel among seven men, and that was not easy.

We got three spoonfuls of jam from a factory in Hamburg each week; when the factory was bombed it was stopped; it was supposed to be made of swedes anyway. We had only been there a few weeks when the German rations were cut by 20%. To help the food supply the Americans tried eating grass, plant bulbs they found under the ground, and even frogs they caught from a stream which ran through the centre of the camp.

Very few of the personal English parcels came through. Mothers sent one a week through the Red Cross. I got one in 14 months. When we were told parcels had arrived in the camp, it was surprising: Canadian, New Zealand, Australian, and American parcels were in abundance, but the English ones were just a trickle; same with letters.

As cigarettes were used as money, and most of the parcels contained 200, the Commonwealth POWs were able to buy food from the Germans and foreign workers. Some of the chaps set up small stalls in the camp where you could buy, sell, or swop anything.

We heard on the grapevine that 50 RAF officers had been shot by SS troops. They had escaped with a lot of others and got caught. Years later, reading a book about it, I learned that on the night they escaped they were delayed because of a heavy raid on Berlin. By coincidence this was the raid in which I was shot down 24–25th March 1944.

Most of the mail, etc., went to Stalag 3 the officers' camp. Some of our NCOs volunteered to go as batmen to the officers so they could make it easier for themselves.

When the parcels, etc., were distributed to the other camps all over Europe, a lot got lost on the way, through bombing. And we must remember Germans were starving as well.

Most of the food that had to be cooked was done on a 'blower' one of the POWs had invented. It produced a fierce heat with remarkably little fuel. The principle of the blower was to create a strong draught of air below the fire by means of a fan driven at high speed. A complicated system was often used to create a stronger draught. We got soup once a day – mostly swedes – and

German coffee twice a day. In between we had to manage with what we got from the food parcels. All we could think of was food. During the time I was there barrels of 'Blue Stalks' arrived; they were like mushrooms and all the colours of the rainbow, gone bad; the barrels of sauerkraut didn't taste very nice, either. There was also fish cheese in fishcakes which smelt awful; most of the lads wouldn't eat them, but I would buy them whenever I had any cigarettes.

At one time things were so bad that we had no food parcels for about three months; we had to manage almost completely on German rations.

The cookhouse was run by the POWs but the guards were always there to keep an eye on things. When the vegetables were peeled the peelings were thrown behind the cookhouse, where the lads were waiting to pick them up; it almost came to fights to get the best pieces, and I was in the middle of it. A surprising amount of good food could be got out of them. To stop a lot of friction each hut had a turn in picking up the pieces.

A box was made with four handles; it was shared between the men of each hut. In the swopping shops you could get almost anything: ice skates, baseball and bat, boots, clothes, watches, cigarette lighters. A lot of this stuff came from Geneva through the Red Cross, some of these men had been POWs for four or five years. It is surprising what you can collect in that time.

Every so often the Red Cross came round to see if we were being treated properly, and had any complaints, not that they could have done anything about it if we had. Each POW was given a diary, a present from Geneva; the Germans allowed this because they could get a lot of information from them.

While on roll-call the guards, who we called 'Ferrets', used to search the huts. Most of the time we spent walking round the perimeter, or, when the weather was good, sunbathing. Of course, we used to play cards a lot, talk in groups about our flying experiences, and of course food.

I met Grant in a different part of the camp; he told me how he jumped out of the plane and managed to get down alright, pretty much the same as me, only he did not land in a dyke. He did have a slight burn on his neck from the burning engines when he baled out.

After a few weeks McDonagh turned up, limping a bit. He told me he had been well treated in a Berlin hospital; the doctor ordered his staff to feed him on chicken soup. He still looked a bit rough and still had his flying boots on even though one of them was cut to ribbons; it did not seem to bother him. He was very cheerful; he still had a lot of metal in him, which the doctor did not take out.

I met a Wop/Ag, Rod Mullaly, who had been a prisoner for three years. He knew a lot about Harrogate, so we had a lot to talk about as we walked round the perimeter. The first two POWs to be shot down, two hours after the war started, were in our camp, Flattery and Booth.

Dixie Dean was our camp leader, a sergeant pilot on fighters shot down in 1942. He and others organised the 'secret radio'; each day they came round to every hut and gave us the BBC news; that is how we knew about the invasion which started in June, and the fifty officers being shot.

The camp was well organised; we even had a theatre; some of the chaps used to dress up as women; it was good entertainment.

If you wanted to go to school you could learn almost any language; the POWs came from all over the world.

I met three chaps from 158 Squadron; they told me there were hardly any of the old crews left; the squadron had almost been wiped out in three months, our flight commander and bombing leader had gone.

Of the thousands of men in the camp, each had an individual story to tell about their experiences; if you could put all these stories together what a book you would have.

Every morning at roll-call, the commandant would be there, counting to see if anyone was missing; he was of the old school, tall and thin – a Prussian. More than likely he had been on the Eastern Front, got himself wounded, and then sent home. He had a limp; I remember once on parade, when he was counting, one of the lads had his hands in his pockets. He came over and pointed to him, and in broken English said, 'you, the cooler'. You couldn't blame him; the Germans were keen on discipline.

McDonagh and Grant used to call round; we would play cards and talk about how the war was going on; McDonagh lost a lot at cards and was always borrowing off me. When we left the camp he owed me five hundred cigarettes; if only he had paid me I wouldn't have gone short of food.

We spent a lot of time in our beds thinking about what was happening back home. Round and round the perimeter we walked every evening until we could walk no more; then we collapsed on our beds. When we got up the room would start spinning. For quite a time the allied forces seemed to be at a standstill; although we got the BBC news as well as the propaganda news from the German guards, it did not help; every now and again we got a German newspaper.

The question was, when were they coming for us? And would it be the English, Americans or Russians? We were right in the middle.

After a while we were moved from the tents into one of the huts, still on the American side. The first day in the hut two Americans walked in and asked if they could start digging a tunnel under my bed; they thought that as we had just moved in the Germans wouldn't think we would be trying to escape so soon. The nickname of one of the lads was 'the mole'; they dug down six feet and along six feet; next day it was all flooded so they gave up the idea.

Senior NCOs were not allowed to work, so we had no chance of getting any food from the land workers, who were mainly Russian and Poles. Some of the chaps managed to get white bread and eggs if they had plenty of cigarettes, but I never got any.

About this time orders had come from German High Command to all POWs that escaping was no longer a sport; all Germany had been split up into zones; if any POW was found in them he would be shot without warning. As all POWs had their photos taken on arrival and were given a number – mine was 3452 – it was easy for the Germans to identify us.

We used to find ways of passing the time; some of the lads were experts at making gliders out of plywood and toilet paper, they flew well, and at odd times used to fly out of the compound, the guards were very interested, and brought the gliders back. It must have been a boring life for them; they were just as much prisoners as we were.

The Americans played baseball all the time. I used to crochet with a needle I made out of an old toothbrush, filing it at the end into a hook. It was easy to get hold of some old woollen garments, I undid the wool and made quite a few berets; a sleeping bag I made out of a blanket, underpants I made out of silk from my flying boots. Time dragged so much it was good to find something to do.

The lice were a lot of trouble; we had to keep searching for them in our underclothes. Every week or so we had to go and be deloused; we would have a hot shower, and our clothes would be put in a hot oven. Dysentery was another problem, most people had it at one time or another. When we first arrived we were told that 40,000 Russians were buried in mass graves nearby, who had died of typhus.

There was an easy way of making a skating rink; it was so cold all you had to do was throw a few buckets of water on the ground, and it would freeze straight away; the Americans had some ice skates.

Outside our hut we had a cold water tap and, surprisingly, it never froze while I was there; each morning I took a shower (if you could call it that). I used to rush in quick and come out just as fast, at least it kept me clean and fit.

One day the Germans called us out on a special roll-call on the parade ground. At each corner was a machine gun with men behind it. You can understand why we felt a little scared.

The commandant stood in front of us and read out a proclamation from the German high command. Because of the way German POWs had been treated out in the desert – they'd been put in chains – reprisals were to be taken against British POWs. There was a rumour going round that Hitler had given orders for all POWs to be shot, and that Himmler had talked him out of it.

On the bottom of our bunks were wooden siats, spaced. On top of these we had a straw mattress; the Germans took these away and we had to sleep on bare boards.

As a diversion from these unhappy events I would like to record at this point the experiences of a fellow POW. He was held at the same POW camps as me until the end of the war.

Miracles Do Happen

At 2100 hours on the night of 24th March 1944, our Lancaster bomber, 'K' for King, took off from our base at RAF, Witchford near Ely, fully laden with an 8000 lb bomb and incendiaries for our trip to Berlin. This was a 'big 'un' and a maximum effort,

with well over 1000 aircraft and many diversions to other lesser
targets. We were due over Berlin in the first wave at about 11.15
p.m. and it was one hell of a cold night. We crossed the coast
at Cromer and turned on a long leg up the North Sea to Sylt,
climbing on track. We crossed over Sylt and turned on course
due east to Stettin and on to Berlin. Over Sylt I saw two aircraft
go down in flames and we settled down to the job in hand.

We turned again on track to cross Berlin from north-east to
south-west – and Berlin is a big city and spread out over a large
area. We were apparently early over the target and anti-aircraft
shells were exploding well below us, a sure sign of night fighters
at our height. We saw the pathfinder markers go down, and
headed on to our point and dropped on given time.

We headed for home, to cross the Ruhr well north, near
Hanover and across Holland and back to base. All sounds very
ordinary, but . . . we were attacked, according to our rear
gunner by a JU88 who split us open with his cannon shells. I
was listening to a Group broadcast at the time, and I switched
over my intercom and heard the dreaded words, 'abandon aircraft'. I forgot to unplug my headset and nearly pulled my head
off, and moved to the rear to find the exit; I opened the door
behind me and the whole area was one huge mass of flames,
bright orange and hot. I closed the door, and went to move
forward, I had automatically taken my parachute from its stow-
age and clipped it on my harness. The aircraft was now perform-
ing the most weird aerobatics and I found myself literally stuck
to the ceiling by the force of 'G'. No panic – but how the hell
do I get out?

At that moment, my problem was solved. The aircraft literally
broke in half and I went into the dark unknown. I obviously
missed the fixed wire aerial and the trailing aerial and lapsed
into unconsciousness through lack of oxygen and the intense
cold.

I came to my senses, and found I was falling through the dark
night and all was completely quiet; I went to pull my parachute
handle, and then panic broke out; it was not there. I was falling
in a straight position, and I looked up above and found, or
rather noticed, my chute unopened and flapping above me on
the ends of my harness webbing. I couldn't reach it. I pulled
the harness down towards me, found my chute, pulled the

handle, and 'plop' – it opened straight away, and I realised my heart beat was, to say the least, very fast; immediately I landed on top of a huge forest fir tree, and found I was tangled up on the branches and shroud. I realised my chute had opened with only seconds to spare and before it could slow my decent, I had hit a tree at something like 150 mph.

I swung towards a decent-sized branch, unclipped my release and started to climb down the tree. I wasn't apparently injured. I came to the bottom of the tree and saw snow beneath me – about a six-foot drop. I jumped, and God, I found I had jumped into a depth of snow which must have been six feet deep. I took stock of myself and realised I was bare footed. My flying boots and socks has been ripped off; I had a packet of cigarettes and an orange in my flying blouse; the juice of the orange had soaked into the cigarettes which were a handful of soggy tobacco.

I succeeded in finding a forest look-out post, about 75 ft high with a ladder, and climbed up to see just where I was. All I could see in the moonlight was thousands of high trees as far as the eye could see, and I could still hear the sounds of aircraft above me – all heading home. I sat and reflected. I reckoned I had fallen about 18,000 ft unconscious and came to just in a nick of time, lucky B. . . . I reckoned also at that time that I must have held the world record for a delayed drop. What a thought!

I walked barefoot in the snow until 5.00 a.m. before I came into a village where I was taken prisoner by the local police. Without any foot-wear I don't suppose I could have got far without severe frostbite. I was taken to a house where I saw that my navigator had been found and brought into the warm. He was terribly injured, poor devil.

I was taken in the night to a military prison at Wurl, and then to Frankfurt Dulagluft for interrogation. Two weeks in solitary confinement on starvation rations, in a room without any light, and finally by cattle truck with hundreds of others to Stalagluft 6 at Heydekrug, East Prussia.

After the war I met my rear gunner, Nick Alkamede, who I learned had fallen out of the rear turret deliberately to end it all, as his parachute had caught fire in the fuselage and he did not want to fry in the plane.

He landed in thick trees and compacted snow and had not broken a bone in his body. He had actually fallen 18,000 feet without a parachute. His story was not believed, but the aircraft remains were searched and his parachute remains were found still in the crash, and his harness was intact. He was given a document by the Germans to state they had found his parachute in the aircraft, all burnt, and he landed miles away.

His story was authenticated. Our other crew members were all killed. Miracles do happen.

To return to the main story, of course, when the officer had finished speaking, almost everybody started booing, but we kept an eye on the German gunners all the time; all our mattresses were put in a separate compound and locked up; it wasn't very nice sleeping on bed boards with gaps in between.

A few days later one of the POWs broke through the wire of the compound and grabbed a mattress. That started a steamroller effect; one after another went in and took one, including me; I think I was about the last going in, and as we were making our getaway a German guard came round the corner with a machine-gun in his hand. I ran as fast as I could expecting bullets in my back. If he had fired he would have been quite within his rights.

We used to get up to all kinds of tricks. There was a hut in the compound where the Germans kept swedes and potatoes. It was empty for most of the time. One chap would walk by and give one of the boards a kick, then someone else would do the same thing; after a while they had knocked the whole side down, then it was not long before the contents were gone; we had to get fuel from somewhere.

When the Russians started to advance towards East Prussia it was time for us to move.

All this time Dixie Dean and his helpers had been looking after us, supplying us with the BBC news; it was marvellous how they were able to hide the radio from the Germans, even though we had searches regularly. Day and night we could hear the big guns going off, and there was a lot of air activity. After the invasion we expected the war to be over quickly. Maybe the way I have explained our activities you might think we were in a holiday camp, but I assure you we were not.

Some of the POWs had been confined four or five years. You

must be mentally affected and depressed after all that time, and have the feeling you are never going to be released; some had young wives and family and did not know how they were being affected by the bombing back in England.

Almost everyone suffered from malnutrition and dizziness. Myself, I was lucky to have been a prisoner for only 14 months.

Thorn and Fallingbostal

Commonwealth POWs left Heydekrug by trucks to Thorn in Poland, but I am afraid some of the Americans had a hard time of it.

They were taken to Stettin on the coast and put into the hold of a ship, packed like sardines; that would have been murder for me. When they got to their destination, they were attacked by the Hitler Youth who had a training camp nearby; some were badly beaten up; the Germans youths were trying to get their revenge for some of their family that might have been killed in the raids. Some Americans were put in dog cages where you could not stand up. Thorn was much the same as Heydekrug – out in the wilds, and almost full of POWs before we arrived.

We were getting nearer to the fighting zone, not far from us was a FW 190 fighter station; they used to shoot up the camp (practice of course).

When we first arrived one of the tales going around was that the POWs were given a peep show by the young girl land workers, mostly Poles, just outside the wire, in and out of the bushes in their underclothes. It was causing such a disturbance that the Germans had stopped it before we got there. Just our luck.

Back home, brother Fred was still flying as a signals leader, living dangerously although he was not on ops. Sister Marjorie was still with her new boyfriend. The Russians were still advancing so we were on the move again; at night you could see all the gun flashes.

We did not spend a lot of time in Poland; the next place was Fallingbostal in the heart of Germany itself. That's when the fun started. This place was in the centre of all the main targets: Berlin, Hamburg, Hanover, Frankfurt, Stuttgart, and many others.

The camp was much the same as the other two – surrounded

by woodlands. The BBC was always available on the secret radio. Although Dixie Dean was our camp leader, Fallingbostal was an army camp. Captains and Majors were in charge. Dixie was only a sergeant; he expected to take orders from them, but not so; as he got on well with the Germans and could speak German he was put in charge of the whole camp.

By this time Halifax and Lancaster bombers had taken to daylight bombing so, with the Americans as well, it was quite a sight.

During the day the sky was blanketed with planes; usually, to get most of the targets, they had to pass overhead. And the night bombing was going on as well; wave after wave of bombers and fighters – anything up to 2000 at a time. We could see dogfights and planes going down, something you could never see back in England.

High in the sky above the rest of the planes we could see the new German jet fighter, travelling at high speed. If the Germans had been able to produce more of these planes the war might have been different. It wasn't – thanks to Bomber Command bombing the factories. Even the Russian planes were about. It was a free-for-all. At night you could hear the planes and the ack-ack guns; at least now we knew the war would soon be over.

After the catastrophe at Arnheim most of the paratroopers who were taken prisoner came to our camp. A lot were wounded in the arms and legs. They had come in gliders pulled by bombers. The Germans were waiting for them. It was hopeless.

Dad before he was married. 1919

Mother before she was married.
1919

Me at 16, I looked about 12. 1938

Sister Marjorie just before
she went to Canada as a
War Bride. 1945

Me, aged 15. 1937

Mother, Fred and wife, Edna, outside Buckingham Palace. 1943

Fred as a Flight Sergeant in the middle of his first tour. 1942

Me, taken at Lossiemouth, O.T.U. 1943

In 1941 all aircrew under
training wore a white flash
in their caps

Dad, night porter, staff painter, air-raid warden at the Spa Hotel, Harrogate. 1940

Fred. 1944

CENTRAL CHANCERY OF
THE ORDERS OF KNIGHTHOOD,
St JAMES'S PALACE, S.W.1.

27th November 1943

CONFIDENTIAL.

Sir,

 The King will hold an Investiture at Buckingham Palace on Tuesday, the 7th December, 1943, at which your attendance is requested.

 It is requested that you should be at the Palace not later than 10.15 o'clock a.m.

DRESS—Service Dress, Morning Dress, Civil Defence Uniform or Dark Lounge Suit.

 This letter should be produced on entering the Palace, as no further card of admission will be issued.

 Two tickets for relations or friends to witness the Investiture may be obtained on application to this Office and you are requested to state your requirements on the form enclosed.

 Please complete the enclosed form and return immediately to the Secretary, Central Chancery of the Orders of Knighthood, St. James's Palace, London, S.W.1.

   I am, Sir,

    Your obedient Servant,

      Lockley.

Flying Officer Frederick C. Bell,
    D.F.C., R.A.F.   Secretary.

Fred and crew member looking pleased with themselves. 1944

Fred's crew on Lancasters. 1943

TELEGRAM

298

RECEIVED

Prefix. Time handed in. Office of Origin and Service Instructions. Words.

52   LONDON TELEX OHMS   21

From

(PRIORITY CC) C W BALL ESQ 18 CHELTENHAM

MOUNT HARROGATE YORKS =

FROM AIR MINISTRY 73- OXFORD ST W 1 PC 338

26/6/44 INFORMATION RECEIVED THROUGH THE
INTERNATIONAL RED CROSS COMMITEE STATES THAT
YOUR SON SGT HARRY BALL IS A PRISONER OF WAR IN
GERMAN HANDS STOP HIS MOTHER HAS BEEN INFORMED

Charges to pay

s.   d.

RECEIVED

POST 👑 OFFICE

TELEGRAM

OFFICE STAMP

Prefix. Time handed in. Office of Origin and Service Instructions. Words.

43   90

From   L-S   199 5:36 STRANRAER 14

To

MR AND MRS BALL 58 RUSKIN AVE ST GILES LINCOLN

= CONGRATULATIONS KEEP IT UP = HARRY

E-CT 58 +

For free repetition of doubtful _____
at office of delivery. Other enquiries should be accompanied by this form, and, if possible, the envelope   ENQUIRY" or call, with this form B or C

Charges to pay

s.   d.

RECEIVED

POST   **PRIORITY**   FICE   No. 7

Prefix. Time handed in. Office of Origin and Service Instructions. Words.

58   134   OFFICE STAMP

om   m

OOT 358 5.25 LI/T OHMS 20

to

PRIORITY F/O F C BALL 29 OTU RAF NORTHLUFFENHAM

= 18/5 HEARTIEST CONGRATULATIONS ON YOUR WELL

DESERVED AWARD = 49 SQUADRON FISKERTON +

For free re   29   OTU 18/5 49 LLLT - + +; ENQUIRY" or call, with this form B or C
at office of: _____ his form, and, if possible, the envelope

Wedding group.
1946

My wife and I
married in uniform.
I was a Warrant
Officer then.

Received my Caterpillar, when back home from Germany. 1945

Caterpillar members, Polish Airforce Club, Nottingham. 1986

Husbands and wives. 1986

8

On the March

At the beginning of April we were told to evacuate the camp as the Russians were advancing again; about 300 were left behind in the camp including my bomb-aimer, McDonagh; when I saw him years later in Canada he said they were hopeless cases, and were repatriated before the war was over.

When we left Fallingbostal we were given one Red Cross food parcel each. I don't know where they got them from.

We had to carry everything we possessed with us, such as blowers and pots and pans made out of old food tins. I had with me a kitbag, a small suitcase, a blanket I had made into a sleeping bag, and one food parcel. Some of us were loaded.

In the American food parcels there was a tin of margarine called OLO; it was deadly stuff; all along the route the lads were throwing them away. It was awful; this was the start of the march which lasted about a month, sleeping where we could. The Germans tried to stop at farms so we could sleep in the barns, but it could be anywhere – in a wood, or in a ditch.

We usually marched for an hour then had ten minutes rest, but you felt worse when you started up again.

There were 12,000 POWs on the march all over Germany in columns of about 1500. Dixie Dean managed to get hold of a bicycle, and he travelled from one column to another, to help out as best he could.

The Germans told us that if anyone lagged behind he would be shot. Dixie managed to get hold of a handcart, which we had at the back of the column, so those who became ill could get a lift, for their belongings, and for those who had collapsed.

The food parcels did not last long; then we had to live off the land – swedes, and sugarbeat, which we tried to fry to get rid of the tarty taste, or anything else we could find.

We split up into small groups. One made the fire, another found wood, and the rest went to see if they could scrounge any food from the farms we passed. We marched about 20 miles a day; the way we went depended on which way the allied armies were moving. We were in a sort of horseshoe. As one of the armies advanced we moved away from them, whether it was English, Russian or American.

Although the guards knew they were beaten, they had to obey orders. The Germans said, 'for you the war is over' and yet we were now right in the middle of it. I must admit the guards tried to do their best for us.

Most nights we stopped at farms with stocks of potatoes in clamps; the farmers were made to open them up. With luck we would get two or three cooked potatoes, a slice of bread and the German coffee. As far as I know the guards had the same food as us.

Most of the toilets that were dug were holes in the ground with a pole across; it took some balancing on them, and out in the open it was a bit breezy. The women workers in the fields used to have a good laugh, seeing a row of bare bottoms in the breeze; in the villages the local toilets were for men and women. I went to one and sat down. Before long an old women came in and sat down besides me; the toilets were long planks with holes along them.

Just before we crossed the river Elbe, which had a bridge across it (but not for long) we saw the Hitler Youth manning the ack-ack guns. One of them shouted 'Achtung, Spitfire'. Two planes were seen high up. The Germans dived into a ditch; maybe they had no shells left.

It made us feel good seeing them run like that; we started singing and tried to walk upright, laughing at them as we marched along. As soon as we crossed the bridge the Germans blew it up; we saw the explosion behind us, which proved the allied armies were very close. (We were to cross that bridge by truck, over a pontoon bridge built by the army after we'd been released.)

Every day was different; we passed airfields with crashed planes all over the place, some looked in good condition; there was probably no petrol to fly them. Even our own wrecks were scattered about. I wonder how many of our lads died flying them. We saw wave after wave of aircraft flying overhead, and the guns going full blast.

One night we were all herded into a wood with the guards all around us. I was expecting to get a nice place to sleep under a tree, with my greatcoat and blanket, but it rained all night and we were saturated.

Several POWs escaped and got back home; it was easy, really; but the risk was too great; it was near the end of the war, and there was too many SS troops about, making a last stand.

On another occasion we came to a farm with a large barn; we were told to move into it; a lot of the chaps climbed up into the loft where most of the straw was. I decided to get nearer to the big sliding doors; I had a headache and didn't feel so good. During the night there was a lot of shouting and swearing going on, the lads were going to the toilet up in the loft, and the wet was coming through onto the people below. They had no choice – it was completely dark and they could not get out. Anyway, they missed me.

By this time my claustrophobia was coming back again; I managed to crawl over the bodies to the doors and gave them a good bang. A German guard came and opened the doors; I held my hand to my forehead and pointed to the floor outside. I lay down; he did not say a word, so I got into my blanket and got some sleep. Next morning I felt a bit embarrassed. The lads had used this place to go to the toilet before they went into the barn. Once again I was wet through. I felt so bad I didn't care.

After about a fortnight of marching, on April 19th, we reached the village of Gresse. Dixie had managed to persuade the commandant to get him some trucks so he could go to Lubeck, where the food parcels were stored.

A few hours later trucks came to Gresse, with a Red Cross symbol painted on the roofs. Word got round that food parcels were on the way, and to Gresse streamed the columns from the neighbouring villages.

There were 12,000 men in that German village: army and airforce POWs

We were given two food parcels each, and told to get out of the village about a mile before we opened them. Everyone was starving and weak, and with all the kit we were carrying, we had great difficulty with them. We sorted out what we could eat at once. Some of the food was thrown away as we marched along. I ended up with one food parcel, a small kitbag and a suitcase – and that was a strain.

Above us wheeled a flight of Typhoons. They were trailing us; we knew they were around as we heard them attacking targets nearby; the next thing the planes peeled off and were attacking us. My group were in the middle of the column; the aircraft seemed to be coming straight for us, and were so close that I dived with two others into a ditch by the side of the track – one man was army and the other RAF. I do not know why, as there was no protection, but I put the case on the back of my head, the kitbag on my back, and the food parcel on my legs. It is surprising what you do under stress.

I pressed my head into the ground as the planes hurled anti-personnel bombs and rockets. I could hear the thud, thud of the cannon shells all around me, and explosions everywhere.

Seven of the aircraft were circling round for another run when the eighth realised their mistake, and one of the pilots waved at us.

How those pilots must have felt knowing what they had done! There were no German planes about; no guns were firing at them; they had no excuse. In a few seconds it was all over; I got up from the ground; the first person I saw was an army sergeant, his face covered with blood, screaming. Carnage was all around me. Shrapnel had gone right through the suitcase which had been on my head.

The airforce chap next to me was wounded in the stomach and looked as if he was dead. I think that shrapnel was meant for me; I certainly had a guardian angel that day.

Thirty three POWs were killed outright; 42 were injured, 22 seriously. Quite a few died later; seven German guards were killed. Some of the chaps, both army and RAF, had been POWs for three and four years. And then to be killed by your own people.

Dixie, with help from his friends, dug a mass grave, and lifted the remains into it. The German doctors did the best they could to help the wounded, but they did not have the equipment; shock and gangrene killed a lot of them.

After this was all over it was back to marching again. Some of the lads, not being used to so much food, had acute diarrhoea and that wasn't much fun as you marched along; at least we were not hungry.

After this catastrophe Dixie asked the commandant if he would give him permission to go through the German lines to try and stop the allies killing our own people; he gave him a signed letter to get through.

He got hold of another bike from a German officer (his own had fallen to pieces). He also promised the comandant he would be back. He took with him an interpreter; it was risky getting through the German lines, as there were a lot of SS troops about who would shoot without warning.

He managed to get through, and was taken to the British army officer in charge; he explained that our pilots were killing their own men. The officer said it was a good job they had been warned as they had another strike on for the next day in that part of the country. The officer said; 'I suppose you will be going home now.' Dixie said: 'No, I promised the commandant I would return. The army man could not understand him (he did not know Dixie Dean).

After that, life seemed pretty much the same; we marched across Luneburg Heath and from village to village; of course, we ran out of food and had to rely on the generosity of the German farmers. Although we were still prisoners we had a little freedom. The only time I had got out of any camp was at Fallingbostal; every so often we had been allowed out of camp to collect wood for heating and to cook with; just outside the camp some trees had been cut down. We had been allowed to cut up the stumps, and had a handcart to take them back to camp; the guards had been with us all the time on such occasions.

Once, when we were near a village, two of us left the column and called at a cottage to see if they had any food to spare; we were invited in and given a glass of what looked like sour milk. Anyway, we drank it; as we were leaving two guards spotted us and pointed their rifles at us. We walked meekly back to the

List of Allied personnel killed by low flying aircraft at Gresse, Germany, on April 19th and 20th, 1945.

POW No.	Rank	Name		Service No.	Nationality
1.	L/Sgt	L. H. J. Goodfellow	RAF	2571861	British
2. 1094.6	F/Sgt	K. Mortimer,	RAF	1431168	British
3. 1093	Sgt	E. Bardsley,			British
4.	Sgt	J. S. Breytenbach, UDF			S. Africa
5. 25505	Cpl	Downie. Cameronians			British
6. 15904	Thore Cple	G. Moir		2874561	British
7. 20386	Cpl	P. M. Paton Blk. Watch		918030	British
8. 430	W/O	J. Gage,	RAF		British
9. 3932/VIII	A.Pte.	R. Woodgate			Australian
10. 29815/VIII	B.	Not known			
11. 25731		A. G. Hunt.			Canadian
12. 26387/VIII		Not known	Essex Scottish		
13. 3263	B.	W. E. Lawton,	RAF	1565563	British
14. 138572	XIA	Not known			
15. 3566.6.	F/Sgt	J. Gibbs,	RAF		British
16. 2121.3.	Sgt	S. J. Wheaton,	RAF		British
17. 918.	W/O	Shierlaw,	RAAF		Australian
18. 39152	W/O	F. B. Duffield,	RAF	647048	British
19. 874.6.	W/O	W. E. Mackenzie,	RCAF		Canadian
20. 13064/VIII.	B.W/O	W. P. J. Watson,	RAF		British
21. 24384	W/O	C. W. Heathman,	RAF	1378655	British
22.	W/O	G. Douglas,	RCAF		
23.		Joyce, Essex Scottish			Canadian
24. 994	W/O	K. A. Fox,	RCAF		Canadian
25. 24510/VIII	B.Sgt	L. B. H. Hope,	RNZAF	R/126002	New Zealand
26. 94110/VII	B.Sgt	Hawkins,	RAF		British
27. 3429/6.	F/Sgt	D. Bauldie,	RAF		British
28. 9669/VII	B.W/O	Clayton,	RAF		British
29. 335/.3.	W/O	W. A. Bosh,	RAF	623752	
30. 143/**	E.W/O	W. A. Bond,	RAF		
31. 512	W/O	McKenna,	RAF	11489	
32. 448		Steel,	RAF		
33. 1615	F/Sgt	F. T. Price,	RAF	150(11)	

All the above were killed outright.

List of men taken to hospital with injuries following the same attack.

POW No.	Rank	Name	Service No.
34. 1256	W/O	L. D. E. Marriott	658181
35. 150831	W/O	C. L. Williams	546575
36. 7769	Cpl	G. Mensies	46196
37. 7769	Sgt	J. Whitehouse	1442553
38. 3002	Cpl	F. H. Surman	VX0250
39. 42771	W/O	C. A. Chambers	NZ416213
40. 89	Sgt	J. Foster	645044
41. 338	AC	J. D. Stuart	5639318
42. 29612	Cpl	R. Richardson	4627848
43. 486	W/O	M. Buchanan	404646
44. 24336	W/O	D. Cotsell	567496
45. 109	W/O	R. Bonson	635808
46. 7798	Cpl	G. Maman	SX4930
47. 8696	—	R. H. Reed	6286955
48. 601	—	Ridgway	338706
49. 199	—	J. Lee	160352
50. 32003	—	Mackay	2930106
51. 3801	—	Turrell	S1054811
52. 78	—	Austin	746906
53. 279575	—	Pix*	2722115
54. 3385	—	Barnell*	1853402
55. 12274	—	A. Brown*	746717
56. 1029	—	G. A. C. Read*	1186489
57. 25604	—	R. R. Toillon*	L.12077
58. 33243	Sgt	Worthy*	5492295
59. 50392	—	Brooks*	622115
60. 431	—	Lowman*	570626

*Seriously injured, some died in hospital

POW No.	Rank	Name	Service No.
61. 46	F/Sgt	I. Farquhar*	710102
62. 23246	—	Walters*	7419
63. 70845	W/O	Coply*	325915
64. 39166	Sgt	Bailey*	922923
65. 14065	Sgt	Gabain*	2360079
66. 315	Pte	Knoter*	787548
67. 29465	Cpl	Glynn Baker*	—
68. 29506	Cpl	Glynn Baker	—
69. 200	Sgt	D. Patterson*	722234
70. 10049	F/Sgt	C. Bolden*	NX9137
71. 3469	W/O	S. A. C. Smith*	180695
72. 9659	Bdr	Lord*	955266
73. 31090	W/O	J. H. Webber*	51205
74. 175	F/Sgt	R. A. Hunt*	1699818
75. 442	W/O	V. Ross*	1111501

*Seriously injured. A lot died in hospital

column. Early on in the war we would have been shot for this: I think by now they had got the message and knew the war was over.

All the time while we were on the march we were still getting the BBC on our secret radio. Grant, my gunner, was with another group, but we met several times on the march. As I have mentioned, McGillivary, my navigator had been sent to No. 1 Officers' POW camp; he missed all the 'fun'.

Fred, my brother, was still flying as a signals leader. On the last day before we were released we were at a farm somewhere in Germany.

I was with an Australian gunner who was almost bald; I bet he gave the wrong age when he joined up.

9

Freedom at Last

We were making a fire out of logs when an army sergeant said: look, there are Churchill tanks coming across the field. I was not sure whose tanks they were but the German guard near us was. He threw his rifle down, took his coat and belt off, and ran as fast as he could. I grabbed his belt as a souvenir. After that it was almost over. They were British tanks of Montgomery's 8th army.

When the Germans started to surrender and were put in compounds, some of the lads wanted to get their own back so they started to collect watches, rings, and cigarette lighters which had been confiscated from us when we were taken.

Things were a bit mixed up after that; I remember crossing the River Elbe by truck over a pontoon bridge made by the army. We were taken to an airfield. Whether it was in Germany or France I did not know.

Large tents had been put up, and inside we had our first taste of white bread for 14 months; it tasted like cake. Most of the men waited outside on the grass for a plane to take them back to England. As usual the Americans were flown home before we were; loads of Dakotas took them away.

Volunteers from the squadrons were asked to bring the POWs back home. I flew back in a Lancaster – the first time I had flown in one. We sat on the floor. It was a bit uncomfortable, but after the last four weeks, it was heaven. We landed at RAF Cosford.

What a scruffy lot we were, but at least we had smiles on our faces.

At this time I had a beard. We had our photographs taken – I wish I had it now. We had to have a medical, and after being briefed, deloused, and given fresh clothing we were sent on leave.

A lot of the chaps had lost a lot of weight, but I was lucky: at 9st. 2lb. I was the same as when I joined up.

Some of the ex-POWs went straight into hospital and were given extra food rations. Most of the celebrations of VE Day were over when I got back. At least I was alive. That was more than I could say for five of my crew. I saw McDonagh and McGillvary before they went back to Canada. They invited me over for a holiday.

Brother Fred stopped flying in June 1945 and was posted to Cardington, working with new recruits. Later he went to Wilmslow, near Manchester, doing the same job. As it happened my future wife did her training there when she joined the WAAFs in September 1945. Fred was an administration officer. He did not start flying again until 1949.

My sister Marjorie had married her boyfriend, Keith, and they had a baby girl. While I was away Harrogate had filled up with Americans. I had had my share of them in East Prussia. Anyway they had all gone when I arrived home.

Keith had bought Fred's motor bike and before he went back to Canada he sold it to me. Sister Marjorie and her pal Betty Dunn were war brides and left England in January 1946. On May 13th I became a warrant officer; not a commission but the next best thing; at least it showed I had worked my way up from the ranks.

A pal of mine, Rennie Claus, who was in the RAF, tried to follow me like Kilpatrick, but he failed to get into aircrew because he was colour blind. One day he talked me into taking him to Blackpool on my motorbike so he could see his girlfriend. On our way back, near Preston, we had a puncture. I took the bike to a garage, and they said they had repaired it, but all they had done was to nip the inner tube and cause two more punctures. They patched them up and we were on our way. It was now nearly midnight and pouring with rain. We got as far as Skipton and the rear tire went flat; we drove 22 miles on a flat tire with Rennie on the back, complaining all the way home. We were out on the moors and I did not want to walk home. The tire was perfect but the inner tube was ripped to pieces.

10

Poems/Articles/Letters

During the lonely hours of waiting in the prison camp to be released many prisoners took to writing poems or rhymes. Some were good. Others were terrible. We had quite a variety to chose from because the American aircrew were with us – and later on we had the army.

We each had a diary given to us by the Red Cross at Geneva which the Germans allowed us to keep. The following poem is a bit of a tear jerker.

Into the Great Beyond

Daylight hours were closing fast
And deadline time had just been passed,
When Halifax S set out on her tour
To a target of industry in the Ruhr;
The load in her belly seemed hard to stand,
But she struggled on to that distant land.

Her engines roared in a mighty song;
With the grace of a deer she winged along;
She rode the sky like a giant bird.
The crew in her hardly saying a word;
Each man had a job of work to do,
And all were keen to see it through.

They reached their goal at the dead of night,
But that was only half the fight;

For what was to come they did not know,
But prepared to deliver that fatal blow;
The bombadier cried 'the bomb doors are open'
And levelled the target true in his sight;
Halifax S had fulfilled her duty, as her load from her belly
dropped through the night.

'Dive to port' the rear gunner cried;
Ere his sentence finished the bombadier died,
For the spitting death of a night fighter's guns,
Had torn the life from out of his lungs.
The mid-upper answered this challenge of death,
but bullets cut short his life-giving breath.
He uttered a curse as he slumped in his seat;
The blood from his body formed a pool at his feet;
The starboard engines were windmilling round,
And the fuel went gushing down to the ground,
But the flight engineer had the job well in hand,
And spoke encouragingly to that small gallant band;
He feathered the engines as calm as could be,
And gazed at his panel for what he could see;
But a burst from the fighter burst his body apart,
And his hands clutched despairingly at his bullet-strewn heart.

The navigator gave a course for his pilot to fly,
As down to the floor he slumped with a sigh;
He mumbled 'Farewell' with his last dying breath,
Then joined his comrades in the 'Chamber of Death'.
The 'Wop' made his way to the back of the kite,
To help the rear gunner in his merciless fight;
The mid-upper gunner he moved from his place,
And noticed a smile on his disfigured face;
He fired a burst at the lurking foe,
Then uttered a cry of pain and woe,
For a messenger of death found a way to his head,
And left its mark of hate and dread.
The rear gunner gave vent to a yell of delight,
As his bullets ripped open the enemy kite;

Halifax S had stood up to the test;
And revenge was paid for her comrades in rest;
The rear gunner slumped forward, his job well done,
The battle was over and all had been won;
Blood from his wounds was ebbing away,
And never would he see the dawn of the day;
The skipper in front had never spoken a word
For a yell of delight was the last he had heard;
The first burst of fire had smashed open his side; And he fell
on his stick which he held tight with pride.
The Halifax S had fought her last fight.
And plunged down to earth in the still of the night.
The spot she had bombed was her last resting place; Her death
had been honourable and not of disgrace.

H Ball ex-POW

People who read this book may think this poem far-fetched, but
believe me, it is not far from the truth.

At this stage I would like to mention the RAF ex-POW Association; The qualification for membership is to have served in any
branch of the allied air forces, and to have been a prisoner of war.
One of our members, Cyril Aynsley OBE, an ex-Daily Express
Reporter, wrote an article describing the Association. The following is an extract from that article:

Because of the nature of the overall war strategy the bulk of the
membership comprises men who were confined in Germany.
They have adopted for themselves the title 'Kriegie', derived
from the German word for prisoner-of-war, 'Kriegsgefangener'.
Prince Philip was elected an honorary member; he said, 'I do
not believe that anyone who has not experienced it can understand what life as a Kriegie must have been like. It is really a
secret society, or rather, a society which shares a secret which
very few others can hope to penetrate.'
The death casualties in bomber command far outstretched
those of any other arm of the services. So the main strand
of the 'Bond' is, gratitude for continuing life, the sharing of

formidable dangers, the hunger, the cold, the degradations, and above all, the gifts of freedom and liberty.

The guardians of these secrets are now greying at the temple and edging into their seventies.

Going back to September 3rd 1939 one of the first POWs, one of a force of Whitley Bombers, was shot down over Wilhelmshaven; among the crew who baled out was an Irishman, Larry Slattery. During the long stretch of his captivity, he became famous for his violin playing; he is dead now but his name lives on; a memorial fund was organised as a tribute to his talent and generosity.

Each individual member could relate a personal story to fire the imagination and certainly none more than the president, James Dean MBE or 'Dixie' as his friends used to call him.

Deans was an NCO pilot shot down in 1940. By common consent he was elected camp leader and occupied this redoubtable position until 1945.

In the early stages he had under his control and guidance a few hundred fellow prisoners; by the end of the war he was the trusted and respected guardian of several thousand.

His task engendered a formidable challenge requiring the tact of a physician, the courage of a solo yachtsman, the wisdom of a philosopher, the resource of an inventor, the nerve of a racing driver, the patience of an angler and the understanding of a priest.

He was privy to every aspect of life in the camps: the escape committee, the secret radio, the code by which military secrets were relayed through letters to the British authorities; the increasing domestic problems of men whose wives had given up waiting and forsaken their marriage. He was, in fact, the buffer between the captors and the captives; he walked a delicate tightrope across perilous years.

His safety net lay in the fact that the enemy recognised his inestimable worth as an ambassador extraordinary.

I myself am proud to be a member of that 'secret society.'

The following is a letter from a navigator who was at 158 Squadron at the same time as me. He was shot down in February 1944, a month before I was; all his crew were killed but he was lucky to escape, although he was wounded. His name was George Barrett.

Dear Harry,

Yes I was pleased to hear from you yesterday; I forwarded your name and address to Ken Holmes, our membership secretary, last night and you will no doubt receive a membership form within the next day or two – I hope the 'White Rose' Branch of the Aircrew Association is quite active. It is now in its third year and amongst the 90 or so members we have people from Ripon, Catterick, Leeds, Selby etc.

I personally do not help a lot in the promoting of its events because I am, with three others, on the 4 Group reunion committee. 4 Group Reunions, every other year in York, attract 380, being the most we can cope with for the catering.

Last year we had people from America, Australia, New Zealand, France and Norway. Amongst those present, 158 had a couple of dozen at their table. The BBC covered the activities of the committee, and the events of the weekend a couple of years ago.

I mentioned 158 Squadron in that particular programme – perhaps you saw it; it was shown a couple of times. It was not until 1980 that I had the pleasure of meeting anyone from 158 – a chap by the name of Pete Skinner.

In Hydekruge, I was in D12 and worked with Dickie Pape on the production of the Evening News – I drew up the heads for him. Met an ex-Hydekruge chap last year by the name of Ginger Furze; we had quite a long chat.

Whilst at Lissett I flew with Penfold, an Australian called Simpson, and my regular crew skippered by W. Holmes. Our WOP was a Newcastle lad, Tony Rogerson. The book, 'In Brave Company', makes no mention of us apart from '6k. 1 POW' (6 killed, 1 POW) February 19–20 1944, at the back of the book.

Bill Chorley did a lot of research for me a few years ago. I lost my log book so he was good enough to search through squadron records to see the trips I had been on.

I look forward to meeting you one of these days, in the meantime, Harry.

All the Best

George Barrett
Good old 158

In this book I write mostly about myself and the RAF. When we left Poland to go to the army POW camp at Fallingbostal in Germany, almost straight away our camp leader, Dixie Dean, took over the camp. Mixing with the army gave us the chance to swop stories about our experiences.

From these meetings I picked up a few more poems, mainly about the fighting in the desert:

The Rose of No-man's-land

There's a rose that grows in no-man's-land,
And it's wonderful to see;
Tho' it's wet with tears, it will live for years
In my garden of memories;
There's one red rose a soldier knows;
It's the work of a master hand;
Midst the war's great curse,
stands the Red Cross Nurse –
She's the rose of no-man's-land.

Libya

Now this place called Libya is a horrible land,
Where there's nothing to see but acres of sand;
The sun is so hot, but the wind, when it blows,
Is sufficient to freeze you from head to toes;
You would be surprised at the tales I can tell,
There's lizards and spiders, and scorpions as well,
But for all that this Libya is a horrible sight,
You will hear the troops singing by day and night.

Somewhere in Egypt.

Out of the starry skies the moon above came shining through,
Sweet memories awaken those days we once knew,
Somewhere in Egypt I'm thinking of you.

You looked so lovely, your eyes shining bright,
Tears that you tried to hide were just a guide to hold you
tight,
Then as we parted you vowed to be true,
Somewhere in Egypt I'm longing for you.

Oh, I've tried to forget all those heartaches,
That my own indiscretion brought me;
But recall only treasures and memories,
For they always remind me of you.
Here in the desert I sing this refrain,
Hoping the day will come when you and I will meet again;
Somewhere in Egypt I'm thinking of you.

Old Iti's Gun

I have no need for women,
For true love can never be found;
I have no use for women;
They laugh at you when you are down;
If she'd been the girl that she should have been,
He might have been raising a son,
You've heard of the place – Bengazi –
Where most of the fighting was done;
'Twas there that a poor British Tommy
Was shot down by an old Iti gun;
Raising himself on his elbow,
The blood from his wound ran red.
Turning round to his comrades,
These were the last words he said:
'Bury me out in the desert,
Under the Lybian sun;
Bury me out in the desert,
My work for old England is done'.

We buried him out on the desert,
With 'Allah' to watch o'er his grave.
His life for old England he gave.
So now that you're back in Blighty,
And the war is over and won,
Spare a thought for that poor British Tommy
Shot down by that old Iti gun.

The Sand Rats of Mersa Matruh

Now you take a trip from Sidi Gabri,
You travel ten hours into the blue;
And when you hear the bombing and artillery,
Then you waken in Mersa Matruh,
I've drunken sand and eaten it in stew,
For there's nothing else a fellow can do;
When a monsoon or sandstorm sweeps the desert;
We get our share in Mersa Matruh;
I'm dreaming tonight of the desert,
And I'm dreaming my darling of you;
And when I hear the call of action stations,
Then I waken in Mersa Matruh;
Once the Iti arrived at Barrani,
Expecting the Axis to break through;
But the Itis were soon annihilated,
By the sand rats of Mersa Matruh,
Now you Germans who have conquered all Europe,
My advice is offered to you;
If you join the army, join the home guard;
Then you won't meet the boys of Mersa Matruh.
Now my story is nearing its conclusion,
And you Germans of who there's quite a few
Whereas your Mothers, Wives, and Sweethearts wait in Berlin.
Sudden death waits for you in Mersa Matruh.

The Gallant Fifth

There's a deed that will live for evermore,
And a story that will always be told;

Of a place in the desert called Side Rezegh,
And men who were gallant and bold;
Of a battle by sons of the pagan veld,
Who fought till the sands were drenched red;
Till their bullets were gone and the battlefield strewn
With the lorries, the panzers the dead;
Of Boer and Britain side by side.
Who fought for the cause of the right,
And the coming years will not obscure,
Their valiant wonderful fight;
They battled Rommel's rumbling hordes,
Till their ranks were broken and gone,
But though encircled, scarred and torn,
They still fought valiantly on.
The stand of the men of the Fifth Brigade
Will live undimmed through the ages,
And the endless veld will ring aloud,
With the saga of soldiers courageous,
And wherever their nameless graves are dug,
That wide expanse shall forever be,
A holy part of South Africa –
A place of sacred memory.

Another poem from Fallingbostal.

To be Remembered

When war is at hand and danger is nigh,
God and the soldier is everyone's cry;
But when war is over and trouble is righted,
God is forgotten, the soldier is slighted.

Arther Fawcett, Queens Own Bays, 10th October 1944

The POW's Dream

The prison gates were open wide,
The peace had come to pass:
All were free to go outside,
And thoughts of home were true at last;

I saw my mother standing there,
Her arms outstretched in greetings;
I noticed now the silvery hair,
It was a silent yet joyous meeting.
The parting from loved ones was over;
No more would a farewell be said;
Then I thought of comrades behind me,
For their peace was shared with the dead;
But faces slowly dimmed away,
My mind confused, What could it mean?
At last I saw the light of day,
And then I knew, it was all a dream.

Thinking of You
Sent by a girl back in England

Thinking of you all the time,
And wondering how you are;
Trusting that you are guided
By your lucky star:
Praying all the time for you,
My secret silent prayer;
Never giving way to doubt,
To fear or cry of despair;
Keeping all the love I have,
For you and only you;
Clinging to my precious dream,
Oh may it soon come true;
And so in all sincerity,
I send this little rhyme:
To say, that I am thinking of you,
Thinking all the time.

A Sandy Grave.

How often do you think, you folks at home,
Of lonely graves without a stone.
Where sleep our comrades brave and true,
Out in the desert past Mersa Matruh?

The raging sandstorms wake them not;
It's cool below, above it's hot;
The desert trails are over for them,
These heroes of ours, these Englishmen
On rolls of honour their names will shine,
And will not dim with the passing of time;
When brave deeds are recalled we shall think about them,
Those heroes of ours, these Englishmen.
So forget them not you folks at home,
As they lay out there in the sun alone,
For they fought for our empire, freedom and you,
Out in the desert past Mersa Matruh.

The Gremlin Mark 1

Here's to the Gremlin we all know on OPS;
Not a bad sort of fellow was he;
In spite of his habit of dancing on props,
And his hideous chatter of glee:
We'll pardon his joke when he hung up the bombs,
But we frown on this habit you'll agree,
Of his howling and smashing o'er the intercom,
Then breaking your pencil in three;
Gumming flies on the perspex,
Scaring gunners with fright,
While they hosepipe imaginary Huns;
Then putting the nose down when skipper wants height,
And attracting the flak from the guns.

These things amongst many were Gremlin's delight,
And he's still working hard I am sure;
I saw one beckoning me last night,
Saying: 'Here comes Les, second tour'.

Dedicated to the Red Cross and St. Johns, Thorn, Poland July 1944

Each life has its crosses, and an airman has his share,
From a shop across the ocean, to the envious Croix-de-Guerre;
There are crosses by the censor, far too many so it seems;

There are crosses in his letters, from the girlfriend of his
dreams;
There's a cross that's worn by heroes, who have faced a storm
of lead;
There's a cross when he his wounded, there's a cross when
he is dead;
But there's a cross of mercy, that quite a few may own,
To the airman it is second, to that of Christ alone.
It's a cross that's worn by women; when we see it we believe,
We recognise an angel, by the 'Red Cross' on her sleeve.

Mother

Some people wish for riches and gold,
And some for the wealth of another;
But to me there's a thing above all that,
It's the best friend of all, your mother;
She goes through life in a cheerful way,
And the worries she bears all alone;
She wears a smile on a troubled day,
Though her heart be as heavy as stone;
She tries her best to help you,
Though your troubles be large or small,
For she is a friend who is always true,
And proved the best of all,
But even she must answer the call,
To live with the Lord free of pain,
'Tis then you miss her most of all,
And wish she was back again.
So never wish for riches and gold,
Nor crave for the wealth of another,
But think of the dearest thing in your life,
And the best friend of all, your Mother.

Extracts from the Volkischer Beobachler, (a German Newspaper)
Fallingbostal, 3rd September, 1944.
During recent weeks the war has taken on a breathtaking tempo,
military and political events following on one another as never
before in the war. Nowhere, however, has the enemy quite been
able to reach the speed for which the German Offensive of '39–

'41 was distinguished. As compensation for this, the enemy rolls forward simultaneously on all fronts. From the Atlantic to the Far East and from the Mediterranean to the Baltic, the god of war has begun his spurt to the end.

Sunday 14th January, POW camp Fallingbostal Germany.

We got up at our usual time, and as the parade whistle had blown, we were going out on parade; Hank called all room leaders together, and told us the Germans wanted us to take out of our barracks, all tables, forms, and mattresses. Seeing as the camp was crowded with newly arrived guards, we thought straight away, another b . . . search; anyway we did as we were told, and after that we went on to the roll-call.

Meanwhile, lorries and carts had driven into the lager (prison compound), and with the help of a few Russian POWs, the Germans proceeded to pile all our tables, forms, and mattresses on to the transport, and took them away, much to our dis-comfort. Of course, after that we began to get worried. On the parade ground we had our usual guards in charge of us, plus four or five guards with machine guns. On parade ground came the lager officer (the camp commandant) and three other officers. We were told to crowd round them, as they were going to give us a speech. All the lads started shouting and ran towards the officers. He started off: 'Due to the disgraceful way that German POWs have been treated in Egypt, German High Command have given orders for reprisals; you who are soldiers know we have to obey orders. The conditions in Egypt were not fit for European peoples, and I hope you will take this in true British spirit.'

He did try to say more but the lads never gave him a chance. They just walked away in disgust. All the time he was speaking the lads were shouting. He mentioned that we would have to live under these conditions for two years. That started it; one chap said: 'that is nothing, look what we have had to put up with for five years', and another said, 'four years'. We went back to the almost empty barracks and had to manage the best way we could.

Greece and Crete

Here we stand in the land of Greece,
Singing for everlasting peace;
Little wonder we have the blues,
With our hearts way down inside our shoes.
KD shorts instead of slacks,
Living the life of a tribe of blacks,
Excepting blacks don't sit and brood,
And wait all day for food,
It was just a month ago, not more,
We sailed to Greece to win the war,
And as we strained beneath our loads,
The Luftwaffe bombed us off the roads.
They bombed us here, they bombed us there,
They seemed to bomb us everywhere,
And while they dropped their loads of death,
We sat and prayed for the RAF,
Yet the RAF were there in force,
All but a few at home of course,
We saw the entire force one day,
When a Hurricane passed us the other way,
One night we heard the English news,
And good old Churchill gave his views,
The RAF is now in Greece,
Fighting to bring us this hour of peace,
We scratched our moody heads in thought,
'Cause of these fighters we saw nought,
And if in Greece the airforce be,
Then where in the cockeyed world are we?
The bullets whizzed, the big guns roared,
We yelled for ships to get abroad,
At last they came and on we got,
And hurried from that cursed spot,
From here we went to sunny Crete,
And marched us off our weary feet.
The food was light, the water scarce,
To us the whole war seemed a farce,
My paybook was behind to hell,
When payday came I said, 'oh well,

They won't pay me I'm sure of that',
But when they did I smelt a rat,
For when, next day, the rations came,
I realised their fancy game;
I spent my pay in food supplies,
And filled the pocket of some big noise,
And when at last we met the Hun,
At odds of thirty-three to one,
Although they made it pretty hot,
We gave those squareheads all we'd got,
And now it looks like even betting,
That I will soon become a Greton,
And live my days in blackest gloom,
On Adolph Hitler's Isle of Gloom,
But the navy came and with shouts of glee,
We all steamed away o'er the deep blue sea,
But the dive bombers came, we all heard the roar,
And I am glad to be in Egypt once more.

Ex-Gefangener's Nightmare
Published in 'The Camp' (a German Camp newspaper), Nov 19th,
1944 Fallingbostal

The village clock struck loud and clear,
It was the midnight chime,
The eerie howl of a dog was heard,
Through a hush of a winter clime,
The eyes of a cat shone brightly,
As it crouched like a beast of prey,
While the dew descended softly,
Ere the dawn of another day;
The silence was suddenly broken,
Like a bolt dropped from the blue,
For a door was stealthily opened,
And a figure appeared in view,
It was clothed in a snowy garment,
Like a wraith from another sphere,
With a step that makes no murmur,
And a candle burning clear,
As the moon from a cloud comes peeping,

We perceived it was a man,
Is it Robbery, Rape or Murder?
We guess at his evil plan,
With a pace that never falters,
He halts at a small clear space,
And a grin of joy spreads quickly,
Upon the age-worn face.
A fire he quickly kindles,
That soon burns red and clear,
And a pot he places upon it,
The contents seem so queer,
Very soon the smell of frying,
Assails the morning air,
And crouching upon his haunches,
Our prowler consumes his fare,
But why this moonlight excursion?
Come, let us rake the past,
And seek to find a reason,
Before our scorn we cast,
It seems that in the World War,
A Prisoner he had been,
This, then, must be a vigil,
Of days that once had been,
Then a voice cuts through the stilly night,
From a window way on high,
'Lord bless my soul he's off again,
Will memories never die?'
Those 'brew up' years in Stalag spent,
Forever will remain,
And once a year when all is still,
He lives those scenes again.

Army. Gnr. Maunder POW Fallingbostal, Germany

Requiem for a Rear Gunner
R. W. Gilbert

Dedicated to my old 'OPO', Sid Fox, late of 158 Squadron, 4
Group, Bomber Command; and all those thousands of fresh-
faced youngsters who got the chop whilst on ops over the dark

and hostile night skies of occupied Europe, 1939–1945. We have
not forgotten you.

The last time I saw Paris
Her heart was far from gay;
Ten thousand feet below us
The sleeping city lay;
The sky was filled with aircraft,
The moon was big and bright;
Two hundred heavy bombers
Were winging through the night;
We'd left our Yorkshire airfield
At Lissett on the Moor;
At half past ten that evening,
In nineteen forty-four;
The briefing room had echoed
With banter and with scorn;
'We're only off to Paris,
We'll be back before the dawn'.

No ribbon stretched menacingly
To Essen or Berlin;
The red line crossed the Channel,
And ended on the Seine;
This ought to be a piece of cake
With little flak to face,
And ere the fighters know we're there
We'll all be back to Base.

We'd had our eggs and bacon,
Our usual pre-op meal,
As each one hid with nervous smiles
The fear we all must feel,
We'd drawn our flying rations,
Our 'Mae Wests', and our chutes,
We'd togged up in our bulky gear –
Long socks and flying boots.

Around the dark perimeter
The squadron buses run,
With dully glowing headlamps,

Blacked out to foil the Hun;
Like Mayfair cruising taxis,
They trundle through the murk,
Taking the restless aircrews
Out to their evening's work.

Driven by young and pretty WAAFs,
Who make our spirits soar;
They drop us at dispersal
And then return for more;
The ground crew have been working
Since early in the day,
To have our aircraft ready,
Our faithful X X-ray.

In black and dark green camouflage
Our Halifax stands there,
Like some great pondering bird of prey,
Eager to take the air;
We climb aboard together
To check our charts and gear,
To give a final polish,
To turrets, mid and rear.

We smoke another woodbine,
The last one of the day,
'We'll see you in the morning,'
We hear the ground staff say;
The skipper starts the engines.
And runs them up, all four;
The might Hercules motors
GIve out a powerful roar.

The oxygen is tested,
We try the intercom;
Although we won't need oxygen
From the height we're due to bomb;
We join our queueing comrades
Around the track;
We know we're now committed,
There'll be no turning back.

Already A for Apple
And B for Baker, too,
Have rumbled down the runway
To vanish in the blue,
The sun is almost setting,
Our take off time is near;
We reach the glass control tower;
A crowd has gathered here.

We turn on to the runway
And watch the Aldis glow;
Of twenty laden aircraft
We are the last to go;
A 'green' gives us permission,
The runway now is free;
We're flying off to Paris
To see what we can see.

The groupie and the Wing CO
have been here half an hour;
The skipper gives a 'thumbs up',
Acknowledged by the tower,
Some sad WAAFs stand silent;
Their hearts are cold with fear;
Their eyes are focused skyward,
At someone they hold dear.

The fire crew and the blood tub
Have everybody in check,
In case we burst a tyre
And fail to leave the deck;
We thunder down the tarmac,
The wheels are racing fast,
Our Halifax is lifting,

Airborne we are at last.
Circling around the airfield,
We slowly gain some height,
The navigator gives a course,
We head south through the night;
We keep on climbing gently,
Till at six thousand feet,

We're flying straight and level,
Our squadron planes we meet.

And soon we're joined by dozens,
Like tiddlers in a pool;
We cross the River Humber,
Change course again at Goole;
Quite soon we're over Lincoln,
Six thousand feet below,
Crossing the 'Five Group' airfields,
With Lancs all set to go.

Tonight they won't be with us,
As on and on we drone,
They'll find some other targets,
We'll do this one alone;
The heavens grow slowly darker,
The moon is still asleep;
The gunners in their turrets,
A lonely vigil keep.

Two hundred fresh-faced pilots,
Stare out with straining eyes,
Watching for other bombers,
Though still in friendly skies,
Two hundred Halifaxes
Are droning on unseen,
Their tracks betrayed by nav lights
Of white and red and green.

Quite soon we reach the channel,
White Cliffs beneath our wings,
Out go those tell-tale nav lights;
We think of many things;
The phosphorescent breakers
Glow silvery and gold,
We see the moon is rising,
The summer night grows cold.

The gunners search increasingly,
No-one can take a chance,
We climb up to ten thousand feet

And cross the coast of France;
Now several probing searchlights
Reach skyward for the pack,
While from Boulogne's defences
Come several bursts of flak.

That silvery winding ribbon,
Etched white across the plain,
Is France's noble waterway,
The widely flowing Seine,
Her bridges now in ruins,
Her river boats no more,
Sail out from Paris playgrounds,
To Le Havre's distant shore.

Touching the edge of Normandy
By Rouen's ancient wall,
Whose enslaved sleeping populace,
Are waiting freedom's call,
In their uneasy slumbers,
How little do they know,
The landings on the beaches,
Have just three dawns to go.

Some kilometers westward
The D Day bells will chime,
As up the fire raked beaches
The allied soldiers climb,
Through searing shell and bomb burst,
To face the evil Hun,
To fight their bloody battles
Till Victory is won.

The gunners in their turrets
At mid-upper and rear.
Increase the frantic searching
As zero hour draws near;
The pilots in their cockpits
Fly on with beating hearts,
While lonely navigators
Pore over dim lit charts.

Bomb aimers lying prostrate
Gaze fervently below,
Approaching Paris' environs
They watch the city grow;
The wireless operators
Sit listening by their sets,
Flight engineers attending
To petrol cocks and jets.

This is the sort of target
We picture in our dreams,
No crashing, blinding flak bursts,
No packs of Huns, it seems;
No Dante's fires like Dusseldorf,
And Essen in the Ruhr;
No desperate trip like Nuremberg,
When we lost ninety-four.

The skipper breaks the silence:
Three minutes now to go,
Pathfinder markers falling,
On railway sheds below,
Suspended in the moonlight,
Long beads of green and red,
All interspersed with flashes
Of brilliant flares ahead.

With bomb doors gaping open,
We steadily press on,
Till Larry's voice announces:
'Left-left a bit – bombs gone';
The skipper shoves the nose down,
Out and away we go,
As smoke and flames gush skyward
From the doomed yards below.

I feel relieved and happy,
The moon is on our beam;
Then suddenly the fighters
Are in among the stream,
Combats break out on every side,
The criss-cross bullets fly,

I see four stricken bombers,
Fall blazing from the sky.

As cannon shells come leaping,
I watch the battle grow,
A Halifax to starboard
Attacks a one-one-o;
I see another aircraft
About to meet its fate;
A fighter closes in on him
– A JU88.

This is no even contest,
No warring of the gods;
Our bullets can't match cannon shells;
We know the desperate odds;
I nurse my four sleek Brownings
With their belts of 303,
And hold them on the 88
That's quietly shadowing me.

With twice our speed and half our size
We're lucky to survive;
The only thing that we can do
Is weave and twist, and dive;
He takes a chancy pot shot,
His shells fall short astern,
He's a little bit too eager,
To see our aircraft burn.

I tell the skipper to corkscrew,
Before we get the chop,
And as we're diving steeply
I watch the fighter drop,
He very quickly vanishes,
Into the hazy air,
And then with startling suddenness
He fires a fighter flare.

Suspended on a parachute,
It hangs above our tail,
Glowing with brilliant radiance,

Making the moon seem pale,
Crouched in my rear turret,
Well, how am I to know,
That the cunning Hun is waiting
A hundred feet below?

We have no under-turret,
No-one can see below,
He sits there as we corkscrew,
Following as we go;
An upward firing cannon,
Close by the pilot's cheek,
Is beaded on my turret,
It's code-named **'Schrage Musik'**.

Where ignorance is bliss, they say,
'Tis folly to be wise,
Though soon I'll face the 'music'
In those unfriendly skies;
We have the flare behind us,
Suspended there on high,
I watch it fading slowly
From the corner of my eye.

Once more the void is empty,
So peaceful and unreal,
I call through on the intercom,
'Regain an even keel.'
'You can straighten up now skipper
We've lost him I believe,
But don't fly straight and level,
Maintain a gentle weave'.

No sign of JU88s –
No M.E. one-one-os
Quite soon now we'll be at the coast
Where the English Channel flows,
I sigh and breathe in deeply,
With ill-disguised relief,
When streams of white hot tracer,
Come hosing from beneath.

My world dissolves around me,
I take a fearful blow,
My legs are ripped and shattered
From that holocaust below,
My Browning guns have vanished,
My chest is torn and red,
My perspex dome disintegrates –
I am already dead.

Epitaph

My brief sweet life is over,
My eyes no longer see,
No summer walks – no Christmas Trees –
no pretty girls for me;
I've got the chop, I've had it;
my nightly ops are done,
Yet in another hundred years
I'll still be twenty one.

11

Postwar RAF

At the end of my leave, June 1945, I was posted to Church Fenton, Yorkshire, receival and disposal. Because my code no. was 41, and they had only got up to no. 36, they would not release me straight away; they asked me if I would like to put in for a commission, but I would have had to sign up for another three years. There was no future in the RAF for me now.

After serving four and a half years – and by the time I got out it was five years – the sooner I got back to civvy street the better.

My next posting was Rudruth in Cornwall, an isolated place like the prison camps I had just come out of. When I reported for duty the officer in charge asked me what I was doing there: 'You, as a POW, should have been released long ago; in any case the station is closing down'.

Three weeks after I left Church Fenton the group number had gone up to 46; as mine was 41 I should have been released at once.

There was nothing for me to do down there, so I spent most of my time in the 'handicraft' section, making handbags. The RAF supplied the leather and tools, showed me how to make them, and that was it. I became quite good at it and took several bags home. I had learnt one thing and that was patience.

After a few weeks I was posted to 16 Maintenance Unit, Stafford, on a motor mechanics' course, which I thought would be useful to me in civvy street. Grant, my mid-upper gunner who lived in Scotland, wrote to me, and said that a friend of his who had the same group number as me had been released, so I went to see the adjutant and asked for my release. He said he was sorry but could do nothing until it came through on DROs (daily routine orders). It did – six months later. As fate would have it, if I had been demobbed earlier, I would not have met my future wife, Doris.

When I arrived in camp I met another warrant officer. He was aircrew but not a POW. When we got our billets fixed up we decided to see what the town had to offer. I had my motor bike with me, which was very handy to run around in. In town we asked one of the locals which was the best pub. By pure coincidence Doris, who had just joined up and had just done her six weeks' footslogging, was posted to Stafford, and had arrived the same day as me.

Doris was with another WAAF and had gone to the same pub, and sat next to my friend and me. My mate soon got into conversation with them. I was a bit shy in those days. I hardly spoke a word, but we all enjoyed ourselves. Then my mate said, 'Can you take Doris back to camp? She can have my seat on the motorbike.' Of course I had no say in the matter. Doris had a pass and I dropped her off at the guardroom, and then went to my section of the camp. That was all that was needed. I fell for her straight away, but I think it was a long time after that before she felt the same about me.

As a WO I could walk in and out of the camp without a pass; all the other ranks had to have a pass.

I asked Doris for a date, and she said yes; from then on, in between her duties, we went out together.

I was a dull person; I did not dance whereas Doris had won prizes at it; Doris smoked and I did not; she was only 18, I was five years older; she was a little on the flighty side, and I was just the opposite. I think it was the motorbike that was the attraction. She told me later she never expected me to turn up for our first date. Anyway, I started my duties as a U/T motor mechanic; as I had no experience, I had to take orders from LACs, who had learnt their trade. The trouble was the RAF took advantage of this. I was really an LAC wireless operator with a WO's rank, learning to be a motor mechanic. But I still had my WO's duties to do (witnessing officer). On pay parades hundreds of personnel; flight sergeants, sergeants, corporals, WAAFS, and Grade 2 aircraftmen, all in rows, waited to be paid. When their names were called out I had to check the pay they were given. It was very tiring on the eyes.

My next job was 'orderly officer' going round the mess and asking if there were any complaints. Nobody told me what to do. If there had been any, I would have had to use my own initiative. In the hangar itself, we had roll-call first thing in the morning; all ranks lined up and their names were taken; the trouble was, I was in charge of the roll-call one day as a WO, and the next day I was in the squad and my name was taken by a sergeant.

Once, when Doris and I came back from a weekend in Harrogate, we were late in getting back to camp, and the sergeant in charge of the roll-call put me down as absent. I was put on a charge and had to go in front of the CO; as soon as he saw me he said, 'what are you doing here?' and then told me to clear off. What most people did not know was that I could not be put on a charge by a sergeant – only an air commodore could put me on a charge or court martial and we did not have one at Stafford.

By this time I was getting a bit fed up; I wanted to get back home and start a new life as a painter and decorator. Doris and I travelled to Harrogate a few times; the weather was terrible during the winter months on a motor bike. I managed to get hold of a 'Teddy Bear' suit. I think it was the inner part of a Canadian flying suit; it fitted from head to toe with a zip fastener. Doris wore this on the back of the motorbike.

Once, when we were near Huddersfield, we stopped at a roadside pub to get a drink; when we came out there was so much ice on the road the bike slipped from under us, Doris fell on her back but the Teddy bear suit saved her. We took a trip over to Wilmslow so I could introduce Doris to brother Fred. Doris did her basic training there.

Most of the work we did at Stafford was done in the hangars, reboring the engines of lorries, Dodges and Studebakers and even working on motorbikes and sidecars. We used to have fun riding them around the hangars; this work would have been some use to me in civvy street.

One weekend in Harrogate when I had had a few drinks I asked Doris to marry me; I did not think she believed me at first and thought it was the drink. Anyway, she said 'yes'. On leave in Wolverhampton I bought her an engagement ring; it was called a double diamond twist.

On one occasion before we were engaged I thought I had lost her. One night I asked her if she was going out; she said, 'I am doing my hair tonight'. The next day she was put on a charge for being out late after midnight with an airman; after a bit of explaining it blew over and everything was alright again.

Doris applied for her demob because we wanted to get married. She was asked to give a date, so she picked a Saturday out of the blue, February 16th, which was my birthday.

We were married in uniform at Knaresborough register office. Within one week Doris was a civilian. I had already got her parents' consent when I went down to London. Doris stayed with her parents until my demob; then we went back to Harrogate to live with mother. Now came the time to forget about the war and think about starting work, and maybe starting a family.

After being grounded for four years brother Fred went back to flying. In 1949 he was posted to Kinloss in Scotland, on a refresher course. In January 1950 Fred was posted to 38 Squadron Luga in Malta, coastal command, as squadron adjutant. In 1951 he was on air traffic control. In 1954 he came out of the service after 15 years; he settled down in Lincoln with his family; he had one son, David. After buying himself an insurance book, he settled down to his new job in civvy street.

12

Civvy Street

In 1946 I started my own decorating business, pushing handcarts in those days. On jobs I did out of town, I used my motorbike with my old kitbag on the petrol tank, with my tools in.

Later on I bought an Austin 7 from my brother, and used that to carry my ladders, etc. In 1962 my son, who by then was 15, came to work for me. After 12 years he started up on his own. Now we had six children, three boys and three girls: Fred, Judy, Lillian, Linda, Stephen, and Robert. When Stephen and Robert were 16 they came to work for me. They eventually went into partnership with me: H Ball and Sons.

Right from the word go my business did well; I had more work than I could cope with; I had to stop doing outside work because I did not have time to do my inside work.

Doris and I took the two youngest boys to Canada, to see my sister Marjorie and family, Loraine and Ron. They were living in Hamilton, Ontario, 30 miles from Niagara Falls. We were shown all the sights there – sights like Crystal Beach, where we had a marvellous time.

We took a trip over to America, to see a pen pal of my daughter, Judy. We crossed the border at Niagara Falls which was the boundary between Canada and America. I was not struck with the journey by Greyhound coach; it was very tiring. We stayed with a Jewish family and were treated like royalty; they couldn't do enough for us. As for New York, we only saw it in the distance. Marjorie lived in a small house, but the grounds were big, eight acres; it was handy for Keith who liked gardening.

Marjorie came over to England twice, mainly to see mother; Keith did not like travelling so she had to come on her own.

Back home again. One day, while working in the garden where I used to live at 51 Wharfdale Avenue, there was a phone call for me; the man on the phone said: 'Is your name Harry Ball?'

'Yes', I said.

'Were you a W/AG during the war?'

'Yes.'

'Well, I am your navigator, Allan McGillivary.'

He had just arrived from Canada with his wife and two children; he was doing a tour of Europe and called in at York, never expecting me to be around; he came over to Harrogate with his wife, and we had a good talk about old times. I asked him if he had heard from McDonagh our navigator who was also a Canadian. He said he had tried to find him but had had no luck. Anyway, he told me what happened to him and McDonagh when they got caught.

I retired when I was 60; that is when I started to think about the RAF again. I was invited down to Hendon to a luncheon given by the Ervin Parachute Company for the Caterpillar Club. Out of loyalty to Mr Ervin, the one who founded the club in 1926, his family decided to get all the Caterpillars together – about 300 at a time – to dinner; there must have been about 10,000 members by now. I met a lot of Halifax flyers, one from 158 Squadron, and a Spitfire pilot who had done 300 sorties.

It was strange to see all those ageing men, most with bald heads like mine; we were all between 60 and 70 years old. While I was there two pilots who had saved their lives by parachute, by ejecting from a jet plane, received their Caterpillars. Someone in the hall shouted 'now that you have got one, flaunt it.' We had a really good time. Both Fred and I had retired and were able to attend the meetings of a lot of these clubs, what with RAFA, Aircrew Ass., 158 Squadron Club, POW Club, Caterpillar Club, Polish Airforce Club and Nottingham & York ACA.

In Famous Company

In September 1982 I was invited by the Aircrew Association to go to a Banquet at the Guildhall, London to honour Sir Arthur Harris on his 90th birthday. He had been Commander-in-Chief, Bomber Command, 1942–45, and the one who organised all the 1000 Bomber Raids

Fred and his wife came with us. Talk about being in famous company:

The Guildhall, where Kings and Queens from all over the world attend banquets:

Sir Arthur Harris, BART, GCB, OBE, DSO, AFC, LLD.

Air Vice Marshal Bennett, CB, DSO, CBE, FRAes Pathfinder Force

Group Captain Cheshire, VC, OM, DSO, DFC, Dam Busters

Group Captain Sir Douglas Bader, CBE, DSO, DFC, I took a photograph of him one and a half hours before he died of a heart attack; it did not turn out too well, though.

Air Chief Marshal Sir Augustus Walker, GCB CBE, DSO, DFC, AFC,

Air Marshal Sir John Curtiss, KCB, CBM, RAF.

Rear Admiral Guerits, CB, OBE, DSO.

Air Chief Marshal Sir Christopher Foxley Norris, GCB, KCB, CB, DSO, OBE.

Colonel McBride, Canadian Adviser.

Air Commodore Probert, MBE, MA, RAF.

Group Captain Laycock, Vulcan Bombers, Waddington.

Group Captain Bygate, New Zealand Defence Staff.

Colonel Alderman Sir Ronald Gardner Thorpe, CBE, TD, DCL, DH.

Lord Mayor of London,

Miss Lettice Curtis, ATA Pilot.

Colonel Walbrecht, USAF, UK.

Wing Commander Squire, AFC, RAF Wittering.

Air Commodore Pack, CBE, RAF Strike Command;

Squadron Leader Jackson, MBE, RAF.

Air Marshal Sir Edward Chilton, KBE, CB.

Group Captain Tait, DSO, DFC, ADC, 617 Dambusters Squadron, 1944.

Mrs Hortense Daman Clew, Belgian Res Worker (helped airmen to escape).
Squadron Leader Shannon, DSO, DFC, 617 Dambusters.
Group Captain Hamish Mahaddie, DSO, DFC, AFC, C, ENG, Afraes Pathfinder.
And plenty more.

Can you imagine me amongst that lot, a mere WO.

When I went to a 158 Squadron 'do' for the first time, it was just after the Falklands' war at Brize Norton. I met my old signals leader. He remembered Van Slyke's crew. I also saw Raymond Lister, who was the spare navigator on our first trip to Berlin; he told me my skipper had a reputation for killing off navigators. Not true, we only lost one.

It was from Brize Norton that most of the heavy transport was sent to the Falklands. We were shown around the hangars and saw all the big planes. We then had our reunion dinner.

The second time we went to Canada we left the children behind. We landed in Toronto where my brother-in-law picked us up. For the first two weeks I passed the time painting the outside of my sister's house. What a surprise we got when we were invited out to meet some of Marjorie's friends. What a welcome when we arrived: across the garage was a huge flag – the Union Jack. At first they thought we might be offended; after dinner we went strawberry picking, and also cherry picking.

Marjorie, the wife and I were asked if we would like to go over to America for the day. We got to the American border, but they would not let us cross. We did not have a visa. As we had been over to America on our first trip, and our passport had been stamped, I thought we would be OK; that spoilt our day. Marjorie, the wife and I decided to go over and see McGillivary in Saskatchewan. We travelled by Greyhound coach through Toronto, Alberta, Manitoba and then Central Butte in Saskatchewan; we travelled for 44 hours, only leaving the bus for food and toilets; we slept in our seats. Marjorie managed to sleep across two seats; she said she slept well.

When we got to Saskatchewan, at Central Butte, McGillivary and his wife were waiting for us. They lived in a typical Canadian-style house mostly made of wood, but large with rooms below the ground level, where it was cooler. The weather was hot most of the time; I kept on being bitten by mosquitoes; I had a repellant but it did not work.

Mac was very good. Marjorie had a pal, Betty Dunn, who came over with her after the war; she lived about 20 miles away in a place called Moose Jaw. We drove through to see her; I recognised her straight away although I had not seen her for 40 years; we were made welcome although she was not very happy; she had lost her husband, and her daughter lived miles away.

Mac decided to give us a tour of at least part of Canada. First to a log cabin which he owned, and then in a bungalow, bed and breakfast.

We must have travelled about 1000 miles, through forests, great lakes and an Indian reservation with all their souvenirs. Mac wouldn't take any money for petrol, etc. although we did pay for bed and breakfast. After we got back Mac showed us around his place – a farm of 1000 acres. He let me drive the tractor around for one and a half hours. Some of the fields were only used in alternate years, but they still had to be dug over to get rid of the weeds. You started in the centre and worked round in circles, until you had covered each field. It was a bit monotonous.

Mac took us around a vinery which had 56,000 gallon storage tanks. The owner of a granary took us round and showed us where all the corn was stored and how all the machinery worked. We were taken to a farm sale. Mac knew a lot of the farmers, and he seemed to take pleasure in showing me round his friends; some had been aircrew back in England. After we had said our goodbyes we took a plane back to Toronto. We did not want another forty-four hours by Greyhound coach. Keith was waiting to pick us up.

Marjorie's son-in-law, Walt, took me out for a drink at the local RAFA club. I told him about McGillivary trying to find McDonagh and having no luck; he thought he lived somewhere in Ontario.

Walt and I were having a drink, when suddenly he left the room. I thought he was going to the toilet; after a while he came back in and said, 'someone wants you on the phone'. It was one of McDonagh's daughters. Walt, off his own bat, had looked up his name in the directory. There were five McDonaghs in the book. He had five children and lived only 20 miles away; we called round at the house where he was living. Mac couldn't believe his eyes when we walked in; he looked just the same – that cheeky grin on his face.

We talked of old times and he gave me a lot of new information about our experiences over Berlin. He told me when and how he was wounded. When the Junkers 88 attacked and fired a burst, he was hit all down his right side. He said he hardly felt that; the fighter came in again. This time he was hit in the same place, and this time, he said, it smarted a bit. Even to this day he has bits of metal in him that move about.

I cannot understand why McGillivary could not find him when Walt found him so easily. Although he looked well I think he had a drink problem, and was also short of money. It wouldn't have been so bad if he had had a house of his own, instead of sharing with another family.

Back home again, our next reunion dinner was at Grosvenor House, Park Lane, London, with Bomber Command. This was the best of the RAF reunions. With Douglas Bader gone, Harris soon after, and Don Bennett a few years later, all the famous names are going.

I am in a once-in-a-lifetime photograph of Sir Arthur Harris, Marshal of the RAF, sitting on a chair, with Sir Michael Beetham, Marshal of the RAF, standing next to him on his right side, myself on his left side with my hand on Harris' shoulder. It was an air marshal who took the photo.

All the famous names were there, including several VCs, one marshal, three air vice marshals, five air marshals, two air chief marshals, a brigadier general, two wing commanders, a major, three group captains, and many more.

In November 1983 we went to the Lords Banqueting Centre, London with the POW Association. When I heard these famous people from America and the Commonwealth countries, speaking from the platform only a few yards away from us, I realised how lucky I was to be there.

We have been twice to Bridlington to the 158 Squadron dinner; as we were only four miles from Lissett we took a bus ride around the old runways; the control tower was still there; it had once been a hive of activity – now it was deserted. I met Wing Commander Calder at one of the luncheons; he was at 158 Squadron on Halifaxes before he went on to Lancasters; he remembered Van Slyke's crew it was good to reminisce and get the 'gen' on what happened to a lot of the crews.

When we were down at Lords Cricket Ground Dixie Dean came over to our table. He was in a wheel-chair. He had multiple sclerosis. His wife came from Harrogate.

Back home with my family, I was still enjoying my retirement, I started painting World War Two pictures, 42 of them to be exact, but that was just a phase. I was getting more interested in the different RAF clubs such as The White Rose Aircrew Ass. York where I met a Mr Barratt. He was at 158 Squadron when I was there; he was shot down in February 1944, a month before I was; we must have met on the squadron; he was the only survivor of his crew. All he remembers is trying to put his chute on. The next thing was there was an explosion and the Halifax split in half, he must have passed out and woken up coming down in his chute.

All his crew were killed; he was slightly wounded. We were at the same POW camps and were on that forced march; he was wounded when we were attacked by our Typhoons.

I found out that a few days later one of the crews we were friendly with had come back from a trip and landed in a minefield; of course they were all killed.

Another pilot, on reaching the English coast, was shot down by a Junkers 88, waiting for some unwary crew; they all baled out and survived. When we went to live in Lincoln we joined the Polish White Eagle Club for POWs and Caterpillars.

A letter from H. N. Mottershead, in charge of the 158 Squadron Association.

Dear Sir,

Many thanks for your enquiry on the reunion of 158 Squadron. It is always nice to hear of 158 types, and although we know the whereabouts of some 400 or so, each year like yourself a few more get to hear about us and turn up. It is nice to know that people are still keen enough to learn about those people they knew almost 40 years ago.

From my book on crews, I see your crew was as follows –

Pilot: W/O A. R. Van Slyke, No. R 121701 RCAF
Navigator: P/O A. McGillivary No. J. 20232 RCAF
Bomb-Aimer: F/Sgt J. N. A. McDonagh No. R139235 RCAF
Wireless-Operator: Sgt H. Ball, No. 1435132

Mid-Upper Gunner: Sgt V. A. Grant, No. 1822923
Rear-Gunner: Sgt K. D. Mardon Mowbray, No. 1323693
Flight-Engineer: Sgt Robert Whitelaw, No. 1562121

And, as you say, 'failed to return' from Berlin on the night of 24/25 March 1944. Unfortunately, although as I have said we know where a lot of 158 bods are, I do not know the present addresses of any of your crew; you are the first to contact us. If, however, you know of any, will you let me know so that I can send them a copy of the reunion gen. If I hear from any of your crew in the future I will pass them on to you.

We normally hold reunions once a year, and as you will see the 1983 reunion will be at Bridlington; 1984 venue to be arranged yet. My W/P was Chick McKinnon, and would be at Lissett when you arrived; you arrived as I had just finished my tour in December 1943 with a trip to Berlin. S/Ldr Sandie Sandall, who was the signals officer at that time, and whom you probably knew, attends every reunion and will be at Brize Norton this time. If I can be of any further assistance to you please do not hesitate to contact me and I will help if I can.

As a point of interest, what POW camps were you in for we have a number of ex-POWs who come to the reunions?
Sincerely Yours,
Bluey, H. N. Mottershead.
PS, Can I have your Christian name please, and if you can remember any of your crew's Christian names, it would help.

This is a letter from Mr Chorley co-author of 'In Brave Company', history of 158 Squadron.

Dear Harry,

I was absolutely delighted to receive your letter in which you recorded a quite graphic account of your final operations with 158 Squadron, plus odds and ends concerning your operational tour.

In the revised account of the Squadron's history I shall certainly include extracts from your most interesting letter. I have looked out my notes taken some years ago when I was first researching the Squadron's records. This is what I have recorded concerning the operation to Berlin on 24/25 March 1944:

Zero Hour 22.30 hours. The attack will comprise 830 aircraft, operating in five waves (the actual number of bombers despatched totalled 810) the Squadron being detailed to fly in the second and third waves.

2nd wave will bomb 22.33 to 22.36, made up from B D E G H L N

3rd wave will bomb 22.36 to 22.39, made up from C K M P R S U V T

In the event R did not take off, so leaving 15 crews as follows:

HX349:G, F/Sgt J. Hichman;
HX340:N, P/O R. A. Grey RCAF; LV790:
L, P/O Lawrence RCAF, HX334:
C, F/Sgt B. D. Bancroft RAAF; LV917:
H, S/Ldr W. J. Weller; HX322:
B, P/O E. G. Strange; LW658:
K, F/O W. A. Hughes RCAF; LV920:
D, F/Lt J. N. Reynolds; LW722:U, F/Sgt A. J. S. Wright RCAF: LV792:
E, F/Sgt G. W. Johnson; LW635:
M, F/Sgt P. Kettles-Roy; LW634:
P F/Sgt S. Hughes; LW721:
S, F/Sgt A. R. Van Slyke RCAF; LW718:
T P/O K. S. Simpson RAAF.

Well, as you know, S was lost, and now that I have your letter I will be able to report what happened. Poor Simpson struggled for home with failing engines and reached the English coast, only to force-land in an off-shore minefield, hit a mine and explode; what a cruel stroke of luck.

Of the rest, well – some survived, but sadly many fell in the operations of April-May 1944 – Hughes S. went down on Nuremberg, Hughes W. A. and Kettles Roy on the second Tergnier raid (both were quite disastrous). Lawrence went down. Strong winds, the strength of which were not forecast, though 742 claim to have bombed in the area of Berlin, however 72 crews never made it home, and though you fell victim to a night fighter, the majority were brought down by the Ruhr defences.

The wind was blowing north to south and many stayed well

south of the track on the home leg, and paid the consequences. And on this note I will close.

And all the best wishes,

Dear Harry,

Many thanks for your recent excellent letter, in which you graphically describe the events of what happened to yourself after landing in Germany.

I shall certainly bring your adventures to the attention of the reader. You mention the forced march at the end of the war; I assume there were several, as such incidents have been reported to me by other prisoners of war.

One such person, George Eastwood, managed to keep a daily record of what happened to his column, and one day I must really get down to sorting out all my rough notes, and type up a presentable copy of this quite remarkable diary. Last week I received a letter from Ron Akerman, a Wireless Operator/AG who was shot down in November 1940 whilst flying 'Wimpys' with 9 Squadron. Briefly, Ron's aircraft was hit by flak near Bremen – he thinks – whilst returning from Berlin.

The flying controls were not damaged, but their fuel tanks were so badly holed that it was quite obvious they would run out of petrol well before reaching home. So, in the vicinity of Alkmaar (Holland), the entire crew baled out. All landed without hurt and were soon picked up by the Germans. Ron and crew went off to Frankfurt, then to a camp up near the Baltic coast, where he was split from the rest of the crew, and like you he spent the last few months walking across Eastern Germany. Well Harry I must close.

As usual, my weekends are all too short to allow detailed replies. I have, in fact, written to McDonagh and hope to hear from him soon. Also, Harry, many thanks for the two photographs; you really captured me well on film – thanks.

I will keep in touch,
Yours very sincerely,
Bill (Chorley)

The Poles told us some very interesting stories. One was that in 1933, before the war, pilots had to do their own maintenance on their aircraft. One Pole, we were told, had crashed in a field in a Fairy Battle fighter-bomber when they were flying low over France, and was then taken prisoner; this was at the beginning of the war. It always gave me pleasure to listen to other people's stories; there was always someone with a different tale to tell.

A lot of the things that we were told, my brother and I had shared the same experiences.

In 1985 we went to live in Lincoln; we bought a nice bungalow in Waddington, almost on the doorstep of that famous RAF station. I felt at home watching all the jets flying over us.

While we were there we went to another Polish club – one in Lincoln, for air gunners. Although the wife and I don't go out very much, every so often it is nice to go to these clubs and have a good natter.

We came back to Harrogate in 1987 to a smaller bungalow which suited us.

All the things that I have been told, and all the things that happened to us, I will never forget. That is the main reason why I have written this book.